MW00799791

# SPIRIT
## GUIDANCE

Vision Weaving with Healing Energy

# SPIRIT
## GUIDANCE

Vision Weaving with Healing Energy

**SARAH MCLEOD**

Copyright © 2020 by Sarah McLeod. All rights reserved. No part of this book may be used or reproduced in any manner whatsoever without the prior written permission except in the case of brief quotations included in critical articles and reviews. For information, address Permissions@CitrinePublishing.com. The views expressed in this work are solely those of the author and do not reflect the views of the the publisher.

Limit of Liability/Disclaimer of Warranty: While the publisher and author have used their best efforts in preparing this book, they make no representations or warranties with respect to the accuracy or completeness of the contents of this book and specifically disclaim any implied warranties of merchantability or fitness for a particular purpose. The author of this book does not dispense medical advice or prescribe the use of any technique as a form of treatment for physical, emotional, or medical problems without the advice of a physician. The intent of the author is only to offer information of a general nature to help you in your quest for well-being. In the event you use any of the information in the book for yourself, which is your constitutional right, the author and publisher assume no responsibility for your actions.

*Author photo by Branden Barber*
*Chakra image by Jerome Cronenberger, 123RF*

**Library of Congress Cataloging-in-Publication Data**

McLeod, Sarah

Spirit Guidance: Vision Weaving with Healing Energy

p. cm.

Paperback ISBN: 978-1-947708-47-1 • Ebook ISBN: 978-1-947708-50-1

Library of Congress Control Number: 2020912900

First Edition, November 2020

CITRINE PUBLISHING

Schenectady, New York, U.S.A.
+1 (828) 585-7030
www.CitrinePublishing.com

# CONTENTS

## FIRST CHAKRA
## GROUND AND CENTER     12

## SECOND CHAKRA
## UNLEASH CREATIVITY     40

# PREFACE

T
HE FOLLOWING PAGES ARE transcripts from Vision Weaving™ sessions with healer Sarah McLeod. By tuning into the unified field—the infinite potential of Universal consciousness, the messages and transmission come through with an infusion of light and healing energy for her clients. During each session, the person is lying down and listening to a music track specifically designed to take the mind offline, their focus turned inward to be in the optimal place of receptivity.

The guidance that comes through Sarah's channel is not only pertinent for the initial recipient but also applicable to each of us to find our way home to ourselves. The words are woven with codes of light and an energy transmission that enables a profound reconnection to Source. Thus as you read these words, you will also be receiving the energy transmission. It is possible that you may undergo some deep shifts in your consciousness that affect your waking reality. It is normal to experience some catharsis as a result of the energy you are receiving. This is the process of clearing out the negative "program" and rebooting your operating system. Just like a software upgrade.

This process can be likened to the scientific term *neuroplasticity*. And while at this point in time there are no scientific studies verifying the healing effects of a Vision Weaving session, recipients have shared that they have had mind-altering experiences that shift old "mindsets," the repetitious, self-destructive behaviour patterns that no longer serve them. Sarah has come to understand that the body's ability to heal itself is tied into the energy imprints locked in the unconscious mind. This is Vision Weaving, the art of transformation—consciously transmuting discordant energetic forms in your unconscious mind. You are literally reshaping your experience of reality from the inside out and aligning yourself with a sacred path.

Receiving Spirit Guidance is a journey of discovery and remembering who we are and what our purpose is here on Earth at this time. Much of this healing journey is about trusting and surrendering to a higher power. Much of this is about self-love. This whole journey is one of spiritual awakening and inspiration.

Your Spirit knows how to heal you. Listening to the messages from your spirit is the key to your healing.

Now is the time to love yourself just as you are.

Now is the time.

—

# Author's Note

IN A SACRED PRAYER circle in San Francisco, I was given the guidance to combine the messages from a number of my client sessions into a book. It was made clear that while the messages were once specifically for the person receiving them, they are now pertinent to the empowerment and healing of anyone else who witnesses them.

To my delight, the spirit guides then showed me that most of the work had been done—in the session recordings, a book was already written to be shared so that others would also receive the healing. After each client session was complete, I felt completely charged and expanded, ecstatic to be alive and to be of service in this way. I stood in deep gratitude, humbled to find myself in this place at this point in my life, where this book is what was asked of me and this was to be my contribution.

It is often difficult to put into words, what I see, feel and sense for a person in a session. I liken it to being shown the holographic energy field of a person and then "instructed" where to shift patterns of discord or glitches in the body's systems of natural flow. Really, I am just listening, watching and being told what to do to support the unraveling of the knots and tangles in a person's consciousness.

The whole foundation of this work is based on the understanding that *energy precedes matter and consciousness precedes energy.* When you shift the patterns of discord at the level of consciousness, it ripples into the physical form and thereafter affects the waking experience of reality. Sometimes the things I see or feel could be considered science fiction or fantasy, but one thing I have come to understand is that, in the realm of consciousness, there are no boundaries, the imagination is the limit, and the "form" that energy takes is unbound by our mental constructs of what is real and what is not.

Being a student of many indigenous teachings, I am also aware of the wisdom of soul lessons and how they present in our lives. Always my prayer is that the person receiving the healing learns the soul lessons attached to the experience they find themselves having, so that they no longer keep operating from the old mindset and habitual self-destructive behaviors.

After having these distant healing sessions transcribed and reading them myself, I became aware that an energy transmission was indeed woven through the words and was activating a spiritual awakening in myself. I found the messages simple and profound in their direction for finding answers to some of life's greatest challenges. Always the essential message is to look within our hearts—and yet sometimes in life, more intricate guidance becomes necessary to point us back to this place. The writing of this book has been a process of mindfully selecting universally applicable wisdom from the transcripts, and then organizing them by themes associated with each of the seven chakras in the human bioenergetic system (and if the chakras are a new concept to you, a brief introduction is provided on page 8). The readings may be experienced in order or selected based on your own intuitive awareness of a temporary energetic block in one of the chakras. Either way, the book is intended to offer just the "word medicine" your consciousness desires. In publishing this book, I am walking my talk of listening to inner guidance and trusting the mystery of the universe to align with my intent of empowering humanity to be the best that it can be. Aligned in mind, body and spirit, our race is capable of such tremendous transformation.

> "We cannot solve our problems with the same thinking
> we used when we created them."
> —*Albert Einstein*

As a matter of responsible practice, I encourage people to not believe anything written in the transcripts here. The words on the following pages are intentionally crafted (by Spirit) to activate you. This stream of consciousness is not necessarily gospel, or even true. These words are delivered in a way that enables the grip of a rigid mindset to jump off the tracks. Freeing your thoughts from habitual pathways allows you to step back and tinker with the cogs that whirl and spin and operate the mechanism of your thinking. Imagine being able to dive into the operating system and repair the glitches and fragmentations. With conscious intention focused on healing and the mind disengaged, the aperture for the presence of spirit opens wide and is palpably experienced." I've found that often it generates some discomfort as feelings lurking in our depths rise to the surface, and it highlights the subconscious programming, like a "subroutine," that creates your reality.

That being said, take what resonates for you and leave the rest. If a passage doesn't hit the mark for you, disregard it. If, however, it sparks and galvanizes a shift in your perspective or a fine-tuning of your awareness, then it has served its purpose. So often we function in our day-to-day lives without even being aware of the background monologue and negative self-talk which, self-defeating and self-destructive, keeps us living in a prison of mediocrity. Awareness is the key to zeroing in on the source of those thoughts, so that we may consciously redirect the inner dialogue to one that is life-affirming and empowering, freeing us to be our fullest, most radiant self.

Consciousness is intelligent and the work of Spirit Guidance is intentionally designed to generate new self-realization in a gentle unfolding. It will always reveal to you as much as you can handle and are able to integrate into your waking life. And yes, most growth is uncomfortable, because it is stretching us beyond the normal confines of our experience. No matter which direction our life is going in, so long as it is familiar we feel safe. If anything in these pages "stirs the pot" and generates a feeling of discomfort, this is progress! It means that it is working.

Love will guide the way. My teacher would ask, "What would love do now?" because in this human form, we are really an endless well of questions about how to "do" life. This question is especially pertinent now when the rules of the game are changing fast.

The word here now is trust. Trust that you've got this. Trust that the universe has your back and that you are worthy. Enjoy the wave. Get up on your board with your loved ones held close and ride that tsunami. Life on Earth is getting very intense very quickly. With the hard lesson from Mother Nature in the form of a virus, she is shedding that which no longer serves her: the dense, destructive frequency that can no longer hold form as she raises her own vibration. It is part of the upward spiral of conscious evolution. Awakening. Into the Light. Remembering.

Talk to Gaia in the months to come. Honor the ancestors of the land where you make your home. Ask them permission to and acknowledge the spirits of the land. This simple act helps to keep the balance. Listen to and respect the teachings of the First Nations people. Their ancestors walked in harmony with the Earth for eons before colonization. They lived in deep reverence of the Spirit realm. In recognizing their part in the manifestation of your waking reality, you work in harmony with Spirit Guidance by expanding your awareness to the energy in your field and remaining attentive to what is allowed in. You become sovereign. You create sacred space. You keep the channel open. The messages can come through loud and clear.

You've got this.

Your body—your incredible sensory apparatus—will show you the way. All those hours of yoga on the mat, of meditation, of prayer and spiritual practice, have honed and magnified that channel of information available to you. Light is information and all of that work has opened your meridians and pathways to give and receive this Living Information.

And here you are.

You might have actually been waiting for this moment for about a thousand lifetimes and here you are...

Your spirit is large and powerful, vast and wise...and it is seeking to enliven your heart and mind and capture your attention in a way that alerts you to the energy that wishes to be unlocked and expressed through your physical form. And yes, it will shake things up in order to do that. Please know that your spirit guides the reading. IT is orchestrating the play of consciousness. I am merely a scribe, in humble service...

SARAH MCLEOD
Byron Bay, Australia
November 2020

# INTRODUCTION

HELLO, DEAR ONE.

Thank you for taking the time to absorb this energy through the written word. It is important to state first and foremost that I ask you not to believe anything that I say! I ask you to examine this book with your own consciousness to see if it rings true for you. Does it resonate in your being? Does it ignite the flame of truth in your own heart? By asking this of you, I am asking you to fine tune your awareness and align it with your own instinct, your own internal compass of what is right and what isn't. So as not to be blindly led by yet another voice in the sea of noise, convincing you that something is right for you, urging you to unconsciously follow, allow yourself to see if your instinct is guiding you to proceed.

Yes? Beautiful. Thank you. And I truly mean thank you. Because when any single human being has a moment of clarity as to who they are, when they recognize and see the majesty of who they truly are, we all benefit. We all heal. We are all elevated. We all evolve. It is a beautiful thing to behold.

It is my intention that, by reading these words, you are activating the will to evolve and awaken deep within your being. With your free will, by your own volition, you are taking the reins of your existence and consciously choosing to reclaim your power.

"Conscious intention colors and moves everything."
—*Master Hsing Yun*

Imagine a tiny little seed with a hard shell that has been lying dormant in the Earth for some time, and now it has been soaked in the spring rain. The water ignites the life force and the nature of the seed sends out a tiny root shoot and a sprout. This seed has all of the information encoded in its DNA to turn into a full-grown plant or tree, given the appropriate environmental conditions and nutrients.

It may be that your spirit, your essence, your truest self is like that seed lying dormant and waiting to be activated to grow into its full expression. If this is true for you, may this be the germination of your spirit!

Maybe you are already aware of yourself as a spirit incarnate in human form. Maybe your spirit is already guiding the way. Maybe the concept of you even having a spirit is new to you and it is hard to wrap your mind around the thought that on some profound level we are all connected, we are all woven of the same fabric, we are all one. Beyond age, race, religion, or gender. Regardless of where you are in your journey, let this be an amplification for your evolution. Let these words enrich you with the necessary nutrients and be the sunlight and the water for the garden of your soul.

As we evolve as conscious beings, we are aligning with the qualities of highest good. These are the qualities of compassion, empathy, kindness, generosity, gratitude, and forgiveness. These emotions are "high vibration" and they are sacred. Many of us have entered the world with the opposite of these qualities imposed upon us: cruelty, indifference, hostility, meanness, thanklessness and blame. All of us have experienced trauma and violation to some degree.

Part of our healing journey and reconnecting to Spirit is seeing the bigger picture, recognizing that our spirit chose to have these experiences in order to learn in the School of Life. No matter how hard or intense the journey, beautiful lessons of the spirit can be born from them. With our own divine will, we can find our spirit, no matter how lost, no matter how trapped or guarded. In the realm of Spirit, anything is possible. Where is your spirit? Is it fully embodied in your physical form? Are pieces of it scattered through time and space? Did it "leave the building" after a violent assault or some damaging, traumatic experience that hurt you deeply? With your will and intention to know yourself as a spirit and to fully embody your spirit in your beautiful human form, you are calling in the sacred. You are calling in a life lived with these highest qualities embodied moment to moment.

It is also important to note that I don't claim to be anything or anybody special or anybody's spiritual teacher or guide. I am a very ordinary person sharing what I have learned from my own life experience. I have been in a place of being so lost, I didn't even know I was lost. I have made mistakes because I am human. I have not only stared into the abyss, I have been at the bottom of it wondering how to find my way. So I know that you can find your way too.

Given the nature of my own story, looking back, it is somewhat miraculous that I am here today. It has been the most magical journey of finding my way into the light. I am frequently humbled by a body that has taken many hard hits. I am ever in awe of divine nature, and always learning in the School of the Great Mystery called life. If these words are of service in assisting you to live a life that is filled with love and gratitude and a new or greater connection to Spirit, then I am ecstatic that I am able to help.

When these visions and messages of Spirit Guidance first started coming to me, I honestly thought I was losing my mind. For example, I would "see" or "hear" something in or about a client that I was working with—I was a masseuse for many years—and I disregarded the messages as passing thoughts...and sometimes questioned the soundness of my mind. But the visions and messages became more insistent until I found the courage to speak and share what I was sensing. Time and time again, I received astonished validation and affirmation from the people I spoke to, who shared the accuracy and appropriateness of my awareness, and so I began to learn to trust these messages.

The confidence and authority in the words on these pages comes from years of working with clients and constant, absolute validation from them in response to their experience. Not once or twice or many times—consistently this is validated. In an effort to value what I was experiencing, I have come to appreciate that there are many different kinds of "extra normal" abilities. And it turns out that I have a whole range of tools in my toolkit, which came to me through a traumatizing and yet catalyzing childhood violation which cracked me wide open. Of course, it took me years to appreciate this—or to understand it. Now I find I am someone who has variants of clairvoyance, clairaudience, clairsentience, mediumship, precognition, telepathy...with an ability to see inside the body as a "medical intuitive." It's not without a tremendous amount of support from many mystics, shamans, healers, spiritual teachers and my own powerful Spirit Guidance that I have reached the place of feeling at home and grounded with these abilities and how this allows me to assist others. For this I am so grateful.

There is now no doubt left in me that this is a real, tangible and palpable way to affect deep and lasting healing and transformation in people's lives. I've seen it hundreds of times. I now know from my own life experience that we have the power to transform our lives with mind, body and spirit in alignment.

I call these healing sessions Vision Weaving because essentially, with your Spirit Guidance, we are weaving the visions that are revealed to me. By tuning into your consciousness, I am able to see the patterns and forms that have imprinted in your holographic energy field.

Traumas and violations create fractures, fragmentations, glitches and twisted knots in a person's energy field, just to give a small example. These patterns manifest as disease, mental anguish, addiction or repetitive self-destructive behaviours. This is the "story" or subtext that runs like a broken record in your inner monologue. These patterns of discord flow in the deep undercurrents of your life, directing the path of the river. A Vision Weaving session is a transformation of the mind, body and spirit. The work is about shining the light into the parts of your consciousness that are in shadow and finding pieces of the puzzle that have yet to be revealed to you. Your own spirit guides each session and reveals what is ready to be absolved and integrated as soul-life lessons.

With Spirit Guidance, we are weaving the threads behind the veil that create the fabric of your waking reality. Often what I am shown in a healing session is incredibly difficult to describe in words and sometimes words do not do it justice. Spirit guidance weaves analogies, symbols and metaphors to create a picture. The words in this book are my humble attempt to translate and convey the kaleidoscopic shapeshifting energy that is presented to me. There are three parts to this work:

- **Recognition:** Becoming aware of the pattern or energy imprint held in the unified field of consciousness.
- **Restoration:** Transforming the energy imprint that is creating the fragmentation or stagnation in the field, thus supporting the flow of energy through the body's systems and assisting them to function as they were designed to.
- **Regeneration:** The flow of energy and our natural state.

If the energetic field of the human body could be seen as hologram, it would give you some idea as to how the information presents itself to me. Woven into these sessions is the knowledge of ancient healing modalities that leverage meridians, chakras and nadis to help define the flow of energy through our forms. I am an avid advocate of any modalities that involve the focus on the breath such as yoga, meditation, tai chi, martial arts and sacred dance. When a person presents for a session who has a practice that involves the breath, their energy shifts effortlessly and easily. Their ability to transform, shift and flow with grace is blazingly apparent! Breath is the key to unlock stagnation. Breath is the key to healing and transformation!

The information in these words is nothing new. Mystics, sages, and spiritual teachers have been walking among us for thousands of years. It is my intention, as you take in the energy from these words, that it catalyzes a resonance in your being and creates an opportunity for you to have an awakening realization of who you are and why you are here. Let it act as a mechanism to activate the evolution of your consciousness, so that you may discover the brilliance of your spirit, the magnificence of your being, and the radiance of love and light at your core so that you may shine.

My teacher would ask us to contemplate: *What is the Grandest Vision of the Greatest Version of you?*

And after years of considering this question (eventually discarding the teenage dreams of the classics: rockstar, movie star and millionaire) I came to understand that the most fulfilling life I could live, the greatest version of me: was the honour of walking the sacred path, expressing my heart and soul through creativity and holding the torch aloft for others to find their way.

So I would ask the same of you now too:

*What is the Grandest Vision of the Greatest Version of you?*

It is my understanding that all of us are a work in progress; there is no end to our betterment or evolution. It's not like you reach spiritual wholeness or enlightenment and then stop. The nature of the universe is infinite! So long as we are incarnate, there is always more for us to know about ourselves, always places for us to grow to and spaces to grow into.

Wherever you are on your journey, welcome!

## Crown Chakra
### *SAHASRARA*
**KNOWLEDGE, CONSCIOUSNESS, FULFILLMENT, SPIRITUALITY**
"I UNDERSTAND"

## Third Eye Chakra
### *AJNA*
**INTUITION, LUCIDITY, MEDITATION, TRUST**
"I SEE"

## Throat Chakra
### *VISHUDDHA*
**COMMUNICATION, EXPRESSION, CREATIVITY, INSPIRATION**
"I TALK"

## Heart Chakra
### *ANAHATA*
**ACCEPTANCE, LOVE, COMPASSION, SINCERITY**
"I LOVE"

## Solar Plexus Chakra
### *MANIPURA*
**STRENGTH, PERSONALITY, POWER, DETERMINATION**
"I DO"

## Sacral Chakra
### *SVADHISHTHANA*
**SENSUALITY, SEXUALITY, PLEASURE, SOCIABILITY**
"I FEEL"

## Root Chakra
### *MULADHARA*
**ENERGY, STABILITY, COMFORT, SAFETY**
"I AM"

# THE SEVEN CHAKRAS

THE WORD CHAKRA IS derived from the Sanskrit word meaning "wheel," and is used to define a vortex of energy above the body, where physical matter and consciousness meet. Much of the work that happens in these pages is the act of balancing the energy of the chakras.

There are seven main chakras that align with the spine and represent different organs, feelings and energy flow. By bringing our awareness to these energy centers, it assists us to recognize where we are feeling blocked or stagnant in our lives and therefore allows us to shift the blockage and create flow.

## The Chakra System

The first chakra, the *Muladhara,* is at the base of the spine relates to our feelings around survival and safety. It correlates to the first three vertebrae, the colon and bladder. It is associated with the color red.

The second chakra, the *Svadhisthana,* is above the pubic bone and below the naval and relates to our creativity and sexuality. The energy of this chakra allows you to let go, feel change and experience transformation. A person with an open second chakra is passionate, grounded and creative. It is associated with the color orange.

The third chakra, the *Manipura,* is at the solar plexus. It relates to our self-confidence, self-esteem and self-worth. It correlates to the liver, pancreas, stomach, lung, adrenal glands, large intestine and the digestive system as a whole. It is associated with the color yellow.

The fourth chakra, the *Anahata,* is located at the center of the chest at the level of the heart. It correlates to the heart, lungs and circulatory system. When open and flowing it allows us to feel unconditional love, compassion and kindness. It is associated with the color green.

The fifth chakra, the *Vishudda,* is located at the throat. It correlates to the throat, thyroid, esophagus and its energy flows depending on how we communicate and speak our truth. It is associated with the color blue.

The sixth chakra, the *Ajna,* is between the eyebrows, on the forehead, and correlates to our eyes, brain, pituitary gland, pineal gland and nervous system. When the energy is flowing through this chakra, it allows us to have clarity and self-reflection. It is known as the "third eye" and when open, it gives an ability to intuitively see with your mind's eye. It is associated with the color indigo.

The seventh chakra, the *Sahasrara,* is located at the crown of the head. It correlates to our spiritual connection to the divine and enlightenment. With this energy flowing we are able to receive the guidance from our spirit. It is associated with the color violet.

Over the years, I have come to understand that my work is largely about clearing the energy of emotional stagnation and mental interference. Every indigenous culture in the world has their stories, dances, rituals and ceremonies that serve to keep the negative forces at bay. In the modern world, this place lacking spiritual awareness, we walk around completely unaware of what surrounds us in the unseen realms that permeate our everyday. We are blind to what we pick up and carry energetically. The Peruvian grandmother shamans call us "contaminated," and by that they mean our spiritual energy fields are polluted.

For the first half a dozen sessions, I find that my work is akin to working in an energy emergency room. The intention of this work, for my part, is to align the person's mind, body and spirit with their heart, so that they can receive their own spirit's guidance, to do so with confidence and clarity—so that they too, may walk the path in alignment with their soul's mission and find fulfillment.

# FIRST CHAKRA
## *Ground and Center*

# BEGINNING

D EAR ONE,
Let us begin with a deep breath…and just let it all go with that deep exhale…

This is something that people do in a yoga or meditation practice. It is the simplest and most effective way to ground yourself and release what you are carrying—in that deep exhale—releasing all that you are holding onto, all that you are dealing with, all that has landed on your shoulders, all that is bigger than you think you can handle, all that is weighing you down….

*Phewwwwwwww… let it gooooooooooooooooooo…*

Make a sound, sigh it out. Underneath the breaths and the sounds, you may find that you touch on the quaky wavering fragility that lies just beneath the surface—and you may find the need to cry…

And if you do find yourself crying, a trickling tear at first that may turn into a deluge of sobs, just let that all out too....

It is good, *better out than in...* because these watery tears have been trapped inside your body as you "hold it all together" under extremely difficult and trying circumstances. It will feel good to let that all *gooooooooo.*

And to this end you can pat yourself on the back for your courage, your stamina, your discipline and your independence as you thread the eye of the needle, through the fire and brimstone, through the Valley of the Shadow...because this is where you find yourself, a Bright Light, a being of the most beautiful crystalline form, in a world where monsters roam and darkness reigns supreme...

Is it any wonder that you attract weird happenings? A Bright Light in a dark, dull grey and heavy world. Like moths to the light they are drawn to you Bright Light...and you shine so very brightly.

I feel your heart now burdened and laden with worry, tangles and threads pulling at you every which way. *Breathe.* Feel the Guardianship. Feel the stewardship of the Legion of Light that is now in your company...

This Legion of Light, call them to you and welcome them in as your entourage—cultivate a relationship with them, just as I have done over a lifetime of practice. Now it is available to you. This teaching came from Peace Mother Geeta Sacred Song, a Mayan Shaman and dear friend. This link of consciousness happening here and now, this communication that is happening in the realm of Spirit, the light and grace is bestowed upon you also. It is available to you, it is available for you to be aware of the company that you keep in the unseen realms—so you may get to know the presence of Great Spirit, God, the Beloved, Creator, the divine masculine and the divine feminine, for each are represented and each brings different gifts...

My sweet, you are an angel.

And you have just forgotten.

But it is not hard to remember who you are when you align your heart and your mind with your spirit to the highest good, and open yourself to receive the blessings and the light and the grace that is available to you when you simply ask for help....

Practice asking for help every day, every moment if you need too! As often or as much as you need in any given day, ask for help from the Higher Power, from the Highest Good. You will be astounded by what appears before you to guide your way forward. And don't discount the little things...we are talking about the smallest bug to the grandest whale, the tiniest shift of light, or a sound, or a tune on the TV, or something a stranger says in passing. The signs are all around. Pay attention.

What is happening is a synchronization. A harmonization. A shifting of your vibration—to resonate and be in tune with all of Creation. And this fine-tuning is like tuning an instrument. As Spirit Guidance clears away the old sticky threads and tangles that lie deep within your heart and that manifest in your waking world as these sticky threads and tangles, you will notice things begin to shift.

They may be small at first, or not. They may be subtle at first, or not.

But they will occur...and your job is to fine-tune your focus to be attentive and to notice little details of synchronicity: doors opening, random acts of kindness, opportunities appearing, debts forgiven, money found, settlements made and on and on and on...

Because really—when you align with the Highest Good and the Higher Power, when you invite that light into your consciousness, that love into your heart—you cannot fail. There is no configuration of your being that cannot be touched by this power.

It is the All and the Isness.

And by placing your being now, here, in the spotlight, you are allowing yourself to be in the focus of such tremendous power...the God Force that flows through as Spirit Guidance.

All healing comes from the Divine, just as the force that animates our bodies and gives us life. By allowing yourself to receive this focus, you allow yourself to be filled up, infused, blasted, and saturated with utter benevolent goodness. There is no space for heaviness here. There is no space for dark forces or lower vibration entities, and they will be cast out and obliterated.

And here is the secret: you are not dependent on me or anyone else to do this. You have sovereignty over your life! You have absolute power over who is housed in your body. You choose moment to moment what energies you let reside in your sanctuary, your body, the temple of your spirit.

*Will I let the angel that I am meant to be reside here? Or will I let the unresolved karmic baggage, everyone else's ideas and judgments, and the weight of their own shortcomings stick to me and drag me down to their low level of existence?*

No, my friend. You are here to shine. You are here to shine so very brightly. You are here to brandish the flame of truth and justice and love and light and grace so that others may find their way, too.

Fear not about all the tangles...these are like child's play for you to clear. Fear not about the dark forces that haunt you...you are bigger than all that. They are just fears, just more projection from others who cannot possibly comprehend the scale of your work here on Earth. All of these tangles, these occurrences, these obstacles, these snags—they will shift as you align yourself with the Higher Power. As you remember to call on It in every moment, as you need.

Pray hard. This is aligning your will. This is exercising your birthright to claim your sovereignty. This is banishing forces that no longer serve you. This is child's play for you.

You have done it all before. This Mystery School called "life" in which you incarnate here to learn is easy for you. Your alignment will open the ancient cosmic library quickly and you will remember. You will remember your role and your place. Pay attention to your dreams. Pay attention to synchronicity. Pay attention to signs, no matter how small, notice the play of light ...by fine-tuning your awareness and shifting your perspective, you are giving yourself new lenses to see the world and thus the entire orchestration of reality. Perhaps a friend calls at the moment you are thinking of them. Maybe it's so completely obvious that you pass a giant billboard with a message as you muse on a problem. When you open yourself to the messages from Spirit, they come in all forms and from every direction. By allowing yourself to surrender, you are freeing your mind and opening yourself to receive guidance from the entire universe.

Fear not, my friend. Great things are coming. Yes, there is work to be done. Yes, there are tangles to be unbound. Imagine that the orchestration of consciousness is intelligent! And that you are only ever given as much as you can handle...it is an unfolding. It is a gradual awakening and remembering, and it is so very juicy and good!

I ask now, in this sacred space, that the soul lessons that you have had to learn from this difficult time, be absorbed and integrated with ease and grace from this moment forward, so that you no longer need to be repeating the same patterns of discord as you engage and life from your own Spirit Guidance.

Blessings to you and all of your family, to your ancestors...

*Yes!*

# RECOGNITION

D EAR ONE,

Thank you for having the courage to dive deeply into the depths of your being.

You have recognized the need for a shift or a change in your trajectory and you are taking the first step to reclaiming your happiness, reclaiming your right to fulfillment and joy. Bless you.

For this purpose, right now it is urgent to enable a *divine intervention* to call back the pieces of you that have split off into oblivion, drifting and lost. This invocation is a calling back of your spirit that has somehow along the way become fragmented and disjoined.

The angels are here: Michael, Uriel, Gabriel, Metatron, Rafael. Call on them in the coming days. It is no accident that you should come upon this guidance. Their focus is mingled deeply in these words.

Do you see yet how powerful you are? You are a great power generator, now recognizing your true source of power and aligning with your heart. The body's physical bigness will naturally shift along with this recognition. The need to carry extra pounds will melt away as you come to trust yourself and your body's inner wisdom.

So there is a message here *to be kind to yourself.* You have mentally beaten yourself up so much over the years, and also have been on the receiving end of verbal and physical abuse—it is time to let that go. It is time to acknowledge yourself as an amazing human being walking the Earth at this incredibly intense time.

Mental anguish—all thoughts discordant with your essence—is what has you carry the extra load. Spirit guidance is gently and surgically untangling the knots in your psyche now. Imagine it as a rewiring of the circuitry, an illumination of the connections and the pathways in your brain that connect deep into your heart.

Your heart, yes…look deep into your heart. Meditate on your heart, feel it, come to know it, study it with your mind's eye: the tissues, the fibers, the valves, the nerve endings, the pulsing of the liquid life force that passes through this vessel every minute of every day. This is the temple of your spirit. The heart is intelligence and as science is beginning to discover, it has a wider and more powerful energy field than the brain. This organ beats steadily over the entire duration of your life and every pulse ripples out into the universe in a wave form that is infinite…it never ends. Your signal, your transmission, is broadcast unto infinity…

So what are you broadcasting? What vibrations are you transmitting? What is the subtext of the unconscious thoughts beating you up inside and denying you the joy that you so yearn for? Do these voices tell you that you are no good and not worthy? That you are stupid, fat and unlovable?

With these words, I challenge these thoughts. I banish them. We banish them. For you are co-creating here. Whether you are aware of it or not, you are the master of your own destiny. And love is the answer. Self-love, self-worth, allowing yourself to love yourself. Filling your cup to overflowing. You are worthy. Yet these words mean nothing until you believe in them with every fiber of your being.

So meditate on the heart and feel the love in you. Generate that with your power, focus that power on yourself. *Love yourself* for who you are, just as you are…in this moment and with all of your imperfections.

I invite you to see how ridiculous humans are, walking around in a skin-bag of chemicals filled with soft tissue, space and water. These sacks are functioning, interacting, sensing, receiving, experiencing… and then there is the constant judgment of the mind that nit-picks and dissects all the little imperfections in the system that don't fit the illusory picture or program of what we think it "should" be.

You are perfect just as you are! How about that? In all your glory! Unhappy, unsettled, discontent perfection! This is where you are at! Recognizing and acknowledging where you are at is critical to being able to shift it, if it no longer suits you.

\* \* \*

You are alive and radiant and experiencing life and your spirit is smiling because it gets the cosmic joke. You have done this before, time and time and time again, and now you find yourself at a crossroads.

"Well, heck, I'm not happy…how do I get out of this rut?"

In the words of my teacher, "Start with where your feet are."

I see you. I see you with such an immense and huge volume of love just ready to burst out of you and share it with anyone who cares to receive it.

Your comparison to others is only more beating yourself up. What if you did it *your way?* What if you were so happy and content in yourself that the people that you interact with every day were *so moved* after their interaction with you that word spread like wildfire and people were falling over themselves to hire you?

Imagine.

No effort on your part, just a pure transmission of genuine authentic love and kindness. People are starving for this! They won't even know why they want to work with you, they will just feel drawn to be near you.

And then after a good day's service, you are then content in your seclusion, absorbed in the things that you love to do, without the distraction of others' energy around you, for you've lost all reason to compete or "do as much as others" to stand out and be noticed in the marketplace.

There is no shame in needing to retreat: it is self-preservation. It is gathering your energy, strength and power by delighting in the things that fill you with contentment. It is resonating, vibrating, filling your own cup with love, so that when you do engage, that love spills over to anyone in your path. Self-love is charisma. Self-love is magnetic. Self-love is inspiring. Self-love is prosperity in every wave, shape and form.

Remember to integrate and if possible, sit and listen to ocean waves that reflect the beating pulse of your own heart.

This much is enough for now.

Bless you.

*Yes!*

# SURRENDER IS THE WAY

D EAR ONE,

It takes me a while to find you right now in a maelstrom of energy masking your spirit. It is as if you are at the center of a hurricane, arms outstretched, blasting the wind in all directions—screaming. This is the energy imprint that presents here, created by your suicidal thoughts, and it seems no one can hear you.

God can hear you.

There is no storm big enough. There is no place God cannot go to find you. There is no cave, no mountain, no ocean, no prison nor is there any corner of the universe that God cannot find your spirit.

Let me repeat, *God can hear you.*

*I* can also see you. How do I, mere mortal human, have an access-all-areas pass? By dying and being obliterated into a billion particles and being brought back. There are no boundaries in the unified field. *All is one.* In fact, *all* of us have an access-all-areas pass. We have just forgotten how to tune into that. These extrasensory skills and abilities are not supernatural or even extraordinary. They are our birthright. This *awakening* that is happening on a global scale is an exquisite and gradual remembering.

As we become aware, we reveal the vast and infinite playground that is the unified field of consciousness. We are all students of the Great Mystery if we choose to learn. We are all architects of reality. As we heal, we give others permission to do the same.

Consider this as a very real possibility:

What if: you give up now, and you have to do it all over again on repeat until you get it?

What if: you took your life and found yourself in more hell than you are now?

What if: ending your life in despair was actually a path of endless pain and suffering? (As distinct from consciously dying!)

It would give you pause, wouldn't it? That you would just have to keep coming back over and over, lifetime after lifetime, trying to find the way through until you finally realize that the way to finally break free is to surrender.

Surrender is the way out of this situation. Surrenders is the way through. Surrender is triumph and victory. Surrender is liberation. Surrender is freedom.

What are you afraid of? Abusing your power? Hurting people? I see how much light you have in your eyes. I see how big you are as a spirit.

*I dare you to surrender. I dare you.*

I am not afraid of madness. I am not afraid of death. I am not afraid of your magnificence. I am not afraid of your power. I am not afraid of crazy or weird. I have seen it all.

*I dare you.*

You can consider it a challenge.

You can consider it a key.

You can consider it whatever you wish.

But the choice to surrender is always there.

Be prepared to witness miracles.

Be prepared to see magic when and if you do.

In the struggle of the self, it is quite the paradox—to claim victory in surrender.

You were not born to play small. You were not born to hide lurking in the depths of misery. You chose this.

You CHOSE THIS.

You came here to remember who you are.

You want to know what the way out of this living hell is?

The only way out—is in!

Surrender. Surrender to GOD, Beloved, Great Spirit, Creator...

Imagine you have chased your tail for millennia, eons, lifetimes... and it will never stop...until you acquiesce to the Higher Power.

I know what it is like to fight. I came in fighting. I fought hard and long. This body has experienced enough pain for a hundred lifetimes from all my resistance, from all of the struggle and fight.

Surrender is your liberation. Surrender is what is being asked of you now. You stand at the crossroads.

I see you. I feel your love and your light. You have a choice. Keep fighting and keep creating Hell. Or surrender and let go.

This is tough love, because you are one tough creature. You can take it.

All I can do is bear witness and pray for your liberation. Pray that you see the light...

May your choice bring you victory.

Are you ready to quit playing small? Are you ready to claim your power? Are you ready to claim your love, your light, your magnificence and most of all, your consciousness?

You have the power to heal yourself.

Be free, my friend.


*Yes!*

## 1 · 4

# PATIENCE, MY FRIEND

D EAR ONE,

The word that comes through straight away is "patience." You are an immensely large spirit squeezed into a human body and the feeling of impatience—of wanting it all to happen now (well, yesterday actually) as you are sensing the potential, knowing in your bones what is possible, complete with the vision combined with the agitation that it is not happening fast enough for you.

And then there's here and now, where you are stuck in a paradigm of conformity and control—and you are itching to get out of it, literally to "get out of it." The desire to get out of it is seductive and ever present, especially since you are surrounded by other people who know of nothing better to do…

There is a distinct difference between you and the pack of friends that want to avoid feeling. They do not have access or the conduit to talk to Great Spirit in the way that you do. My own dabbling with mind-altering substances at an early age I can now attribute to the yearning desire to find connection to Great Spirit. To know myself as a spirit, to be reunited with Source, to feel heaven on Earth...I was searching for that without knowing it. I was looking to find the pathway home.

I am a great advocate for modalities and therapies that open your mind and expand your consciousness, as long as they are done in a sacred way or with a guide who is properly trained and able to hold space with the highest intentions. And it is in no way the right path for everyone. Some of my most profound healing has come from the teachings of plant medicines in the care of indigenous elders. With sacred space and the guidance of elders, I have been able to access and clear memories and traumas that were locked in a vault and buried so deep that I would otherwise not have been able to find them.

Many indigenous cultures have used "medicines" to connect to Great Spirit for thousands of years. These sacred roads are different and distinct from our culture of mindlessly numbing-out on substances. One is done in reverence and prayer, the other.is about disconnecting from uncomfortable feelings.

*It is human nature to want to alter our experience of reality.* In my experience, altering your consciousness in anything other than a sacred, intentional, guided and protected way, only creates fragmentation by scrambling your thoughts and connection to Spirit. Think of one as trying to find your way in a thick, gray fog, while with the other you have a shining light emanating from within to guide your way forward.

Peace Mother Geeta Sacred Song once told me that the greatest thing you have is your clarity. If you are mindful in all that you do, you cultivate and foster your clarity. We live in a culture where we are *encouraged* to cloud our judgment and thus our moral compass; it is no wonder so many feel so lost. When you have acute clarity and your focus is sharp, then your very essence, your presence, your radiant spirit shines through everything you do. You have a sacred path and you know how to find yourself in your center, so in this way you model—to anybody else who knows you—the way to find theirs.

If you think of yourself as a leader and a role model, perhaps this will alter your desire to join the mob; the seductive lure to get smashed and obliterate your clarity keeps your vibration mired in the web of illusion. You will continue to weave invisible threads of delusion all the while convincing yourself that you can "handle it" and you've "got this."

It takes an *enormous* amount of courage and bravery to face the world clean and sober. Because not only do you then have to deal with your own madness (your thoughts jumping all over the place), but you have to FEEL….and feelings can be painful and uncomfortable to say the least. Let your ability to FEEL be the thing that you foster and cultivate. Because as you allow yourself to feel, you gain the qualities of compassion and empathy, kindness and consideration for others around you. Everyone around you benefits by your willingness to feel your sadness, your being lost, your confusion, your anger, your happiness, your joy—all are tied into the web that you weave with your thoughts.

Taking drugs to get "out of it" separates your head from your emotional body, so that you effectively cut off the connection to your empathic self—and this is a most vital piece of who you are, because without this you are just another crazy robot who seeks to dominate and control. Most people who walk around separated from their emotions or their bodies are consumed by greed or fears or the ego that leaves them wandering in the endless labyrinth of chaos and despair…

May today be the day you find courage and bravery. Being clean means being real with yourself. Being clean means feeling things you may not want to feel. Being sober means feeling the agitation and the discomfort and the restlessness…but it also opens you to feel the higher vibration emotions like joy, happiness, ecstasy, bliss….

Imagine yourself high on life and your happiness being self-generated. What mastery is that? What sovereignty over your own being. It is a major milestone on the journey of life to reach a state of peace and equilibrium but it requires dedication, devotion and *patience*.

Because as humans, we mess up and we make mistakes and we shoot ourselves in the foot. And *if* we have our clarity while we do all of that, we can learn from it and move on—as opposed to making the same stupid mistakes over and over and over again until they get louder and louder and LOUDER and start to scream at us with pain or ultimately take us out.

If it ever arises, heed the fear of death as a warning.

Use it to sharpen the tool called *clarity*.

Awareness is needed for any of us to survive these next few years as the energetic debris flies at us from all directions. Consider yourself in training for a great competition. This is consciousness training and the opponent is your shadow self. Learning to flex the muscle of your consciousness can only be done with clarity and awareness; substances and distractions dull your senses, dull the blade of your consciousness.

Ask your body—is this medicine? If it is, then yes, take it with reverence and respect. If not, then leave it. Does your body lean towards it? Or is there a natural repulsion. You can do this with ANYTHING—food, relationships, decisions, etc.

Patience, my friend. Practice patience. Part of your luck is that you are in the right place at the right time and when all of your ducks are in a row, KAPOW! The vision will be born…

*Yes!*

## 1 - 5

# HOMECOMING

EAR ONE,

A deep and saturating peace is emanating from your core, so congratulations are in order. There is a recognition in your being that you have all that you need right here, and it is timeless. You are tuning into that essence of you that is beyond the restrictions of time and space…it is flowing, it is joyous, and it is free.

Yet I see a jolt in your heart—a parting from a loved one. It's a little bit like the ground beneath your feet became slippery without them there. Remember that Spirit is anchoring you, grounding you, strengthening your root chakra into the Earth so that you are carried by Pachamama, Gaia—the Earth herself is your foundation and support ad you are connected to her.

We ask you to breathe into that grounding cord, breathe into the Earth. Pray to Earth Mother to carry you both safe and bring you safely home. Remember, she is the wind and the water and the earth and the fire…all of the elements that run through your body that are mirrored in microscopic detail in your body's systems and organs.

What heals this jolt will be a return to your native land, if not physically then in your mind's eye. Watch for your spirit animals along your path. They will appear to guide you, bring you messages. Listen to the whispers in the wind, see the light dancing on the water. There is much power encoded in the landscape and unbeknownst to many it is from the vibration of the land itself that the formidable power of a nation arises. The ancestors laid many threads of prayer and song lines over eons, bridging the waking world to the spirit world and walking with us for those who have the inner vision and inner hearing to listen and see.

If you can, exchange and carry a talisman with a loved one before parting. It could be as simple as a stone you find on the beach or a piece of jewelry; infuse it with your love and affection and hand it to each other before you leave. It will strengthen the link, the telepathic bridge that spans beyond space and time. You will continue to journey together, although not in the physical, and it will heighten your ability to astral travel. Your spirits will dance and you will know… the togetherness is palpable, distance means naught.

There is a wave or current that comes through your being in your native place, a strong emotional current that will surface for you to experience, heal and let go. It may come upon you in a wave and by allowing it to flow through you and ground, you are reconnecting a circuit that was like an antenna gone askew and receiving fragments of information and feedback. A deep healing that is going to take place while you are here. And I suspect that upon return you will feel even more like yourself than before you left.

It's as if this antenna has been picking up fragments of signals for eons and messing with the clarity of your channel. It will become apparent through your journey home, which is multifaceted and multidimensional. Many things are clicking into place.

I see you kissing the ground, so to speak, like your native land is welcoming you home. You bring with you all your newfound wisdom and awareness. Be sensitive and responsive to the spirits of the land...

Deer medicine comes into play. Gentleness. You are being asked to find the gentleness of spirit that heals all wounds and connect into your sacred mountain of serenity! The people you will meet and the experiences you will have are creating you as more of Who You Are... shaping you, constructing you, forming you...after your phase of restoration comes an active momentum that is engaged and vibrant, attentive, aware.

Shine on...


*Yes!*

## 1 - 6

# JOY INFUSION

EAR ONE,

Spirit Guidance is pointing to a time in your life that you experienced pure unadulterated joy: giggling, playfulness, being happy for no apparent reason, carefree and open. You're quite young, two to three years old. You remember this, even if the memory is not conscious.

Right now we are imprinting that joy, that vibration into your holographic energy field so that it is not buried in a vault, but in your immediate field—palpable, present and rippling into your physical form so you receive this joy-infusion into your cells every day.

Life turned sideways after that age…what happened thereafter? It's as if reality fractured and became stormy, quenching this joy in this lifetime. But it was never quenched beyond the ability to be reignited. Rather it was diminished and went into hiding; the little light beacon that you were fled in terror and hid, cowering. Was their violence? Verbal abuse? Did the parents split and remarry? Or check out?

It is essential to remember that your essence, your spirit, your True Self is this magnificent radiant strong and powerful light, worthy of joy and happiness. It chose the life that it did because it knew you could handle it, and it knew you would have the tools and the guidance to unravel the tangles that would assist you to come home to yourself.

Inside there is a little child with a cheeky grin, waiting to come out and play. This child has a smile on their lips and skip in their step because this being is lit from within and looking for someone to come share in that happy place.

This little one's countenance is beaming right now, because already there is an inner knowing that the heavy darkness and fear that was clinging and entwined in your system can be dissolved. You know this from firsthand experience now. It is not a concept. It is real. And it is directly proportional to your capacity to transmit and hold love. There is only up from here. There is only more of Who You Are. There is only expansion and discovery as you shed the layers to reveal the shiny jewel of a spirit that is You.

Because quite frankly, you radiate so brightly that in your image your facial features disappear in the transmission of light. Welcome home! It feels good to have you back! This is your natural state—all the rest of it has been a good show, a great character.

You may feel like you are stepping out of an old costume. People will look at you quizzically and wonder what is different about you. There is a glint in your eye that sparkles with your knowing that *anything is possible*.

*Yes!*

# BE STILL

D EAR ONE,

At the moment, I keep seeing a loop like a rope coming down over your head. Similar in shape to the pink breast cancer awareness ribbon, but in reverse. And it looks like if it got pulled it would become a noose! So we are going to remove that along with the feeling of being restrained in some way. For from that feeling of restraint, resistance has been brewing...

Part of this dynamic is that your burning passion to express as a powerful being in the world has been accompanied by an itchiness to take the reins, exacerbated by feeling stuck in the routines of day to day.

It's hard to be in a worldly "routine" when you're accessing lifetimes of experience, because the world's pace is kind of slow in comparison, and you already can sense, see and feel your impact in the world as an energy force. Right now, you're biding your time. Crossing your t's and dotting your i's can get kind of tedious and the suppressed passion can transmute into this squirming, itching, desire to jump out of your skin, to just go do something crazy to shake it all up and make things interesting.

For example, you ask, "*If I poke here…what will happen down the line?*" The tremendous lesson being learned here is patience. Because deep inside you know there is this epic adventure to be had and you're thinking, "Let's get on with it already." But keep in mind that patience is a quality and a practice and a super-über important virtue to cultivate. Because without it down the line, you will be jumping ahead on the wrong beat or putting your foot in it, literally and figuratively, because you are preempting things people are going to say or intuitively knowing what somebody is going to do…

When folks do this, people don't feel heard or acknowledged and there is a door that closes in their mind to possibility in relationship with you…you are invisible.

So the patience that you are fostering now—even though it may feel challenging to sit still and do what is being asked of you—is all about right timing. And it's all about synchronicity and being in tune with all of nature, your nature. It's about knowing when to speak and when to listen. Knowing when to act and when to be passive. Knowing when to express your big, bright shiny self and when to be humble and mild.

Energetically, the loop that you showed me at the beginning can also turn into a snake and feel kind of suffocating. And any time snake medicine shows up, it can be worked with as a "dark" force that suffocates and poisons, or it can be a force of transformation. So the choice is up to you. It's a very powerful medicine; in fact, Amazonians regard anaconda as one of the top three. In any case, right now is an opportunity to transform a negative situation into a positive one but being mindful of how you respond or act. In support, the guides are clearing out the channels up the spine so that the energy can flow from root chakra to crown with no glitches...

Part of learning patience is the practice of stillness. If you feel the need to fidget and wriggle, this is an area where you can really put your focus and attention, knowing that it is building a reserve of power in you, just the practice of being still.

See if you can take ten minutes a day to sit in meditation and still-ness. By doing this, you turn the suffocating snake into the powerful force of transformation. And instead of jumping in and being slightly out of sync, you will find that your timing is immaculate and that all things flow to you and around you in a harmonious way.

Patience, dear one! All good things in right timing.

And as you emerge as a leader, be mindful that words of encourage-ment and support serve others to be their best self. Empowering others *feels* good. When you start to see the ripple effect that your actions and words have on others, there is a sense of fulfillment and gratitude that has no other way to be earned. If you hunger for the feeling of reward, know that those rewards are feelings and qualities that you are cultivating in stillness. Contemplate these wise words your soul has heard before: "When you have mastered stillness, the universe is yours."

This is a reiteration of that message to you. Practice being still in the mind. The simplest mechanism of meditation is to focus on the breath. If you are just beginning, see how many breaths you can count in and out with pauses in between. At first it will be maybe one or two! See if you can get it up into the hundreds. Just watching and counting your breath...the best possible use of time!!! Because it hones your awareness and flexes your patience muscle, which gives traction to all of your creativity down the road.

*Yes!*

# SECOND CHAKRA
## *Unleash Creativity*

# THE ART OF TRANSFORMATION

D EAR ONE,

In this moment, it feels like a "force" wrapped around you is interfering with the transmission of light and love. This force is feeding on heart pain and angst that you felt recently. When you are in that state, and not numbing it with some kind of drug, you emit a certain vibration that attracts energetic vampires. By tapping back into that particular emotional wave pattern of angst—*bam!*—you can feel the force present in your field, feeding on that emotion. It takes the shape of a kind of serpent, like an anaconda, whose presence in your field is not to be judged as a bad thing, but as a lesson. As you find yourself feeling these emotions again, tune into the snake…ask it what its message is for you. You may not get a response right away. It may come in the dreamtime, or an "aha" moment, or the actual sighting of a snake in the waking world.

Generally, the snake represents transformation and kundalini awakening. Its movement is serpentine, winding, meandering like a stream, like water. It sheds its skin to grow bigger and you can imagine that its new skin feels pretty raw underneath, fresh and tender to the touch...

Always the presence of negative forces are lessons for us to examine and learn from. Their presence presents us with a choice: they bring our attention to an aspect of our healing journey that we need to examine. Does it serve you? No, it does not serve you to have it entwined around your energy field...it's better to allow it to meander straight on out of your form.

Dance the snake. Dance the angst and the heart pain out of your body. Thank it for its lessons and messages and let it go. Feel the opening of the energy centers in your body as the energy rises from your root to your crown. The snake is also very sexual energy, so given the nature of your past and the wound that you have been carrying, it is appropriate that this being would show up in your field to get your attention you and bring you lessons.

Snake medicine people command absolute respect—some fear the Snake as many snakes are venomous. Hold this medicine as a symbol and precious gift of transmutation and transformation....and know that by being aware of its presence and working with it rather than being prey at its mercy, you tap into its extraordinary power.

Use that power to transform yourself. Transform your pain, transform your wound, transform your heartache and anxiety into joy and laughter and happiness—you have the power. You know what to do. It's not to say there won't be moments where you are feeling lost and overwhelmed and scared and isolated, but you have just proven to yourself that you will come out the other side. That you are strong enough in your own sense of self that you will look to the positive tools in your tool kit to pull you through.

*You never have to go down the path of self-destruction again.*

Yes, there will be triggers and this is good! Celebrate the triggers that are clearing out the lingering "charge" that lays the tracks you've been walking on, on autopilot, automatically. Once you are aware of the charge and are able to diffuse it, then you can lay your own tracks. You can choose the path you walk on.

Congratulate yourself for the amount of strength you have...what a warrior! What a heart! That it can feel all that pain and angst and suffering and sadness and rage and still come out the other side feeling joy, happiness, and so much love! Thank you, heart. What a great heart you have.

And now, as it has taken so many "hits" and been dealt so many blows, Spirit is offering you an upgrade! This heart has wings—this one has golden energy and has angels tooting their trumpets, flying all around you—this is a heart that you are worthy of, and is worthy of you because you have proven yourself through some of life's most intense lessons. You have hung in there and persevered, and even if it was only a tiny glimmer in the darkest hours, you hung onto that spark of truth and emerged victorious.

This is the jackpot of merit points and life experience, the resolution of karma. Congratulations. You have attained a certain state of being that can take lifetimes to achieve. Allow the knowingness of this to flood your entire being and saturate it with peace. This is the reward.

If you feel dopey or heavy in the next few days, this is a saturation of light in your cells, charging them, infusing you. Let yourself sleep longer, if you need to.

It is done.

Nurture yourself in the next few days—be very kind and gentle with yourself. You have a new heart, one not so susceptible to attack.

*Yes!*

# RECREATING YOURSELF

DEAR ONE,

I am reminded of a story from my own journey to share with you. And that is a friend of mine who is incredible psychic (barely functioning in the real world), who reminded me that if I this were a few hundred years ago and we were living in the circle of a tribe, that I would have been recognized from an early age, singled out and taken into training for being a seer and oracle, shaman and healer. I would have been taught the ways of the sacred path from the beginning, and would have been cultivated to then work with the tribe as an adult.

As it happens, you and I were not born into a time that recognizes or fosters those talents and abilities in its youth. And so as "sensitives" we were cast out into the world of madness and mayhem just as our peers were, only it affected us differently from everyone else. Like moths to the light, people are drawn to you, enchanted by the bright shiny energy field that you inherited in this lifetime.

In the ideal fantasy scenario, there is a school for people such as you and me where we are trained and knowledgeable about our gifts and abilities. Instead we floundered around here and learned through mistakes what works and what doesn't work, sometimes at tremendous expense.

While the school I dream of does not exist at this moment in time for any mainstream access, it is in formation in my imagination and, God-willing, will come into being for our future generations to understand how to co-create reality with Spirit and bring forth harmony and balance for all to benefit.

Really, the school of life and shaping reality is the school of mastery of the Self. The wisdom of this school is woven through the fabric of reality and all the voices of the mystics, sages and gurus, oracles and seers over the eons of time.

What if in your seeking, you had found what you were looking for right now? And it was here and now in this moment, alive, aware and radiant. And what if mastery of the Self was allowing your awareness to stay in the present moment of witness consciousness? Be detached from the story and the drama and the identity of your character that is full of beliefs and judgments and ideas about being in control and holding the reins of your experience.

What if your healing journey was one where you surrender your life to God? It instantly lifts a huge weight off your shoulders, doesn't it? The recognition that there are some things far greater than your ability to handle or "figure out" releases the parameters of your life to infinite possibility. Anything is possible when you surrender the journey to God. When you align your prayers and intentions with the Higher Power, you tap into the vast, holy sacred place, the Source of all of creation.

Trust that healing will show up in myriad forms and in multiple facets of your experience. It is multidimensional, fluid and beyond space and time. Do not limit the flow by judging the way it comes to you. If there are tears, let there be tears. You may need to cry a river of tears. You may need to cry an ocean. Maybe you are crying for all of humanity while you are at it. Maybe you need to cry for the animals and children and trees and, and, and, and…on and on it goes. Every time you allow the tears to come, you are healing yourself. You are allowing the flow. You are engaging the alignment of your being with Source consciousness.

And one day you may find that you are done with tears for the moment. And that there is beauty in the quiet moments after the "rain" has come, when there is a rainbow and a softness to the Earth that has just soaked in the life-giving liquid light. Your body can reflect that too.

You are showing me that your energy field today is like a Picasso painting, fragmented and distorted…from the impact of trauma, yes, and also from aspects of lifestyle. Spirit is swirling your field into a giant vortex kind of like the cosmic washing machine and recreating the "picture" or hologram or blueprint of your form that is blinking back online. This is a huge energy to call in—so if you feel exhausted in the next few days, know that you have effectively taking yourself "offline." This is no small task to achieve. The spirit guides are orchestrating the healing and directing the show.

So the fact that you are ready to do this already shows great progress to me and an innate ability to recreate and redesign your "self." Your Spirit is strong and powerful, but you know this already.

The physical act of writing or keeping a journal is essential to allowing you to process all of this on an intellectual and emotional level and also to share your story. There is the gift in all of this, that your experience—your soul's evolution through the most intense circumstances—lights the way for others who are lost to find the way home to themselves. What could be more rewarding than your light guiding others out of the darkness? Who better than you to allow this to flow through you?

And even if you feel like you are still fragile and at the mercy of intense energy and emotions, know this deep in your bones: Spirit has shown me the vision of your triumph. And I anchor that into reality with my prayers added to your intention—you too are now supported by the "spiritual back-up team" and the legion of light that I have learned to hold in my field as my company and my entourage.

You have literally recreated and reconstructed yourself as you've read this. Please if I may recommend that you read on to allow the work to continue…

And I will finish today by quoting my teacher, Master Charles Cannon: "Everything is appropriate, everything is just as it should be. You are right on track, you couldn't be more on target if you tried."

*Yes!*

# Preparing for Birth

*Note to the Reader: This particular session was for a woman preparing to birth a child, it is metaphorically relevant to birthing any co-creation.*

D EAR ONE,

We begin with the Reiki symbol of beginning. You show me the laying on of hands upon your womb—the message is for you to lay in bed at night and flow this energy to your creative center, inviting in the spirit that would like to be embodied and would be lucky enough to come through you and into form. And so we are aligning in consecrated space to create the sacred container for a being that is so wise and so blessed to come into the lives of two beings already walking the sacred road.

We begin with a prayer for this spirit to come into a body that is healthy and whole and for the Mama to be, to be healthy and whole throughout the time she is expecting. A sensitive and curious spirit is waiting for the "right time"—I see the stars moving like the cogs in a giant clock to click into alignment and create a channel of light for it to flow into existence.

The same could be said with your current creative endeavor. There is a piece you have needed to absorb in your life, an experience you have needed to have, for the wisdom and knowledge to come through for it to be completed. It will be like finding a missing puzzle piece— you know, the satisfaction of finding the last piece to complete the picture is like a victorious "aha" as you put it into place.

So here's a gentle reminder to not beat yourself up about it not being done yet, and to refrain from entering the endless mind loops that we can get into about "why hasn't come to fruition?"

Because it is happening in divine timing. And yes, here is a prayer for the feeling of fulfillment and satisfaction that will come when it is done (it is so close!), the sense of accomplishment, the patting of yourself on the back...all of which you can practically taste because you are so near.

With this, I am reminded of Lao Tzu's words: "Nature does not hurry, yet everything is accomplished."

Sometimes it is challenging when you have cosmic vision and can "see" ahead to the big picture, and yet you are functioning in a human reality with curve balls coming at you from all directions. Everything always takes more TIME than we would like! And at some level of existence, in an alternate dimension, we all have omnipotent powers to manifest instantaneously at the mere flicker of a thought and so our humanness gets frustrated when it doesn't happen in an instant!

Ah, yes...the cosmic joke. And with this, a prayer for feeling ease and grace to have the space and time to create art each day, with another quote. This one is from Ralph Waldo Emerson: "Life is a journey, not a destination."

It is so easy to get fixated on an outcome, a goal or desired result—and yet the soul lessons, the delight and the joy is in the journey itself. With one foot in front of the other, we go up and down, sideways, inside out, and back to front. Sometimes the path has us be a discombobulated mess! And yet with each step forward, we find puzzle pieces that help us see more of the whole picture. Finding those puzzle pieces is like finding treasure!

So knowing that each step *is* the treasure suddenly brings a sense of wonder. What is going to happen next? There is an expectant delight in wondering what is going to happen today.

So yes, there is a desired outcome… let us hold intention for your creative project to be finished! Let us hold the intention for you to carry and birth your first child! Let us hold the intention for your loved one to find healing, to see the light, to have a safe and sacred space to figure it out and find the way home to himself.

Take time each day to add fuel to this intention, giving gratitude for each of these things as if they already existed. This gratitude opens up a spaciousness and capacity in your field for them to take form. Aligning with me here and now in the presence of Spirit Guidance and the Legion of Light, I can feel the particles of consciousness, the currents in the field, moving and shifting to open the aperture, to plant the seed in the realm of pure potential…

*Yes!*

# THE ART OF MANIFESTATION

D EAR ONE,

The word "balance" is the seed of this reading and here is the vision I see. Imagine you are looking at a wall that is made of liquid. When you poke your finger into the wall of liquid, it creates a ripple effect in the liquid and a bouncy kind of sound effect. You've placed the written word "balance" into the surface and it is swirling and rippling through the whole plane.

By giving it voice and speaking the word, you are orchestrating and directing the flow of energy into the transparent screen, membrane or veil that separates the conscious from the unconscious realm. It is rather like throwing a penny into the wishing well, charging your shiny coin with the intention, infusing it with your aspiration, and releasing it into the depths of the unknown.

What will come of the wish? That remains to be seen. But suffice to say that the act is a way to interface with the unseen realms and this, my friend, is the basis of the ancient art form of manifestation:

releasing your intention into the depths for it to ripple out into the universe.

The key to this ability to conjure from nothing (dare I call it "magic"?) is to build the energy and once you have ceremonially released it, to let go of any attachment to an outcome.

If you remain attached (hopeful, charged, expectant) then it can't fully immerse, disperse and take form in the ethers. While you remain attached, there is a thread that links the thought and intention to you and with that link, it is tethered and anchored *without* release into the great cosmic expanse. Practicing the conscious act of "letting it go" allows your intention and prayer to fly free, unfettered, liberated in the cosmic intelligence so that the Universe, then, can shape it and give it form to be born into reality.

Perhaps it will look differently from how you imagined it? Perhaps it will appear and present in a way that you could not have fathomed. Because with true release, it will return to the waking world with a shape and form whose design is fashioned in the womb of the unknown, in the giant melting pot of Creator…and it will return to you in the most magnificent way possible, when you least expect it for you to experience the utmost delight at its manifestation.

So here's to letting go! Here's to planting the seed for balance and now releasing that intention and prayer into the unknown.

Aho!

Now I see your energy field swirling, and turning and spiraling all around and I am reminded of a vision I was shown for myself one day—of an old wise Chinese martial artist master reminding me how to balance on a board that sat across a ball.

Perhaps you could train your brain and muscles to remember? You could hold onto your walking frame while you stand on foot to foot. As you get stronger you could even stand on a balance board? (Having a person with you at first is recommended.)

You do remember. Your body remembers. Your body remembers strength and vitality. Your body remembers balance. It is as if the oil is switching on the blueprint, the cellular memory of normal function. It is a blessing indeed, and I pray that it becomes more easily available to everyone. Yet it begins with you.

And now, as the beautiful harmonic resonance of the OM vibration ripples through your energy field—there is more activation, more strength, more power to you...more engagement with the life force... amplification....

*Yes!*

# HEALTHY DETACHMENT
# AND GROUNDING

D EAR ONE,

The spirit guides want to reframe your thoughts about the relationship with your ex (yes, the one who just popped into your mind)—they are asking you to hold it as a necessary divergence to gain perspective. Rather than wrapping yourself up in guilt or going into a tailspin about it, hold it as something that you chose to experience in order to "see" and feel what you needed to process in order to fully heal in this lifetime.

Whenever there is an enmeshment of energy with another person, it is difficult to have this greater perspective. In a relationship where each person is drawing on the energy of the other to feel whole, there is a co-dependency—and that co-dependency opens the door to fear of abandonment and fear of losing the things that you think make you strong.

In truth, your strength and your power can only be generated from within. If you are leaning on another to feel it, then it is fleeting and illusory and not likely to remain in your life. Whereas if you tap into the vast cosmic well within you, there is an unlimited supply of strength, courage, self-love, and empowerment—whatever quality you need in the moment is available to you. So consider this for a moment: you intuitively knew that you needed to detach from this person so that you could tap into the well within yourself.

And thank heavens you did. Planet-wide, everything that has lurked beneath the surface is coming up to be experienced. For those that haven't done the work of examining their shadow, the shadow is in their face, creating havoc and angry meltdowns and disruption or for many humans—insanity. It is almost as if we have opened Pandora's box and all of the darkness and evil is now flying around us, and at the bottom of the box all that remains is hope.

So for those of us who have managed to hold onto even a thread of light, and you have—it is the thing that will carry us onward. For those who are caught in the tangle of energy that is surfacing as chaos and disruption, it will act like a tremendous elemental force. Whether a tornado, hurricane, tsunami, earthquake or wildfire—it is sweeping the landscape of our psyches, purifying and raising the foundations to rubble, washing away the debris. Now is the time to meditate more than ever, if only to hold the witness consciousness, to breathe through the chaos as it surfaces, and to let the emotions flow through us rather than sweep us away. It is even more challenging when we see our loved ones suffer and struggle mired in a world of illusion, an illusion of their own making.

In whatever storm you may be weathering now, practice the art of remaining in the center of your being. You become the eye of the hurricane—absolutely still—surrounded by a giant vortex of energy hurling debris every which way.

Walk barefoot on the earth. Spirit here grounds your feet. As you move through your day, allow the energy to travel down your legs and ground it. Breathe and ground the energy though your body. Allow any chaos that has entered your field to ground down, down, down through your hands and feet into the Earth. Your spirit knows how to do this and so does your body—it is in your blood very strongly.

Bless you, dear heart—good work.

And as my teacher would say, "Meditate, meditate, meditate...."

*Yes!*

# THE HEALING BEYOND FEAR

D EAR ONE,

Today I was shown a schism in your energy field in the shape of a large S or a serpent, the top of the S passing through your neck and the middle through your midriff and the bottom tail passing through your shins. This energy force is cutting through your field so that it is creating a distortion or an inability to be in alignment—it is kind of separating your head from your heart, and both from the path you walk. The serpent is wrapped around your throat.

And this all presents as a curse laid upon you once upon a time... or you may have been the one who cursed another (and you didn't know about karma at the time).

Either way, you are now paying the price. Either way, you are dealing with a disjointed and fragmenting force in your field...

But the message today is one of hope. And this reading is just for you to acknowledge that you're not alone, there is help out there and you have called upon it…in your darkest hour. There is a legion of light that is coming to aid you, to carry you and hold you and give you a glimmer of inspiration to carry on.

As noted earlier in these pages, the snake *also* represents the ultimate catalyst, the kundalini rising, the shedding of old skin…so as much as recognition of the serpent energy often brings a negative judgment, be aware that it also is a powerful medicine that brings rebirth and transformation!

By being aware of this medicine and working with it, rather than allowing it to dominate and severe and strangle the life out of you, you can seek to learn from it and understand it and allow it to work its magic. Like any life lesson or challenge or obstacle that presents as a "demon," once you have learned the life lesson that allows you to evolve as a spirit, you will find that demon will transform into an angel. There is a beautiful depiction of this journey in M.C. Escher's drawing *Angel-Devil*…look it up online. Ultimately all the dark and the light is embodied in the one whole circle and there is balance. Darkness defines light.

So as you find yourself in the darkness, how is this defining you? It is taking you into the depths of despair, so that you may know the polar opposite, the grandest joy….

See yourself as fully healed. See yourself as radiant and flexible and pain-free. When you find yourself despairing, catch those thoughts and with your pure, unadulterated willpower, turn that despair into gratitude. Gratitude for being healed. Gratitude for your life. Gratitude that you are free of pain.

No matter how bad it gets, you still have your will and your consciousness and you can wield that to summon the vision of yourself as healed by transmitting the vibration of gratitude.

Universal Law 101: when one expresses and feels and transmits gratitude, the universe will respond to match and create that in your reality.

Breathe gratitude into your cells and repeat:

> *I am grateful here and now that I am healed, that*
> *I am full of joy, that I am free of pain. Thank you,*
> *Creator, for this incredible miraculous healing.*

YES. Feel it, breath it. Live it. Call it into being. Here and now.

And allow the tears to flow…there may be tears from a bottomless well and you may wonder if they will ever stop. The tears are healing and they are allowing your energy to move.

And with your soul's permission and on your behalf, I am asking for the curse to be revoked and lifted throughout space and time across all dimensions and I hear a resounding "YES!" Feel the serpent loosen its grip and shimmy right on out of there! Now the curve of that S is a smaller waveform and in alignment with your spine and can ground from your root to your crown, allowing the energy to flow.

When you are lying in bed, visualize the energy meandering from your root chakra and out through your crown in a gentle oscillation of movement. Yes, breathe into this visualization this week…there is a giant spirit of a being inside of you that is strong and bright and powerful and cracking out of your shell.

I often wonder if a butterfly going through metamorphosis is an uncomfortable experience. I can't imagine that turning from a fat squishy grub into a delicate creature with wings and fine legs is without effort and grunt. Or maybe it is asleep through the whole process and just wakes up one day and it is done. Wouldn't that be nice?

Let your bed be your cocoon. Your mind is in need of much sleep and rest while you morph. At this point, your worst fear passes through your consciousness.

And what of them? Look at that. Examine that. Feel it. Acknowledge it. Because the fear that has lurked in you for eons is now looming over you and staring you in the face. And if you deny it, it will run the show, and in that way be a self-fulfilling prophecy. It is important to recognize and acknowledge the fear and shine the light of your consciousness on it. Fear is slippery and illusive and cannot hold form under scrutiny. Once you lock coordinates on your fear and allow yourself to experience it, it will dissipate and dissolve. It can not maintain its composition in the light. The nature of fear is to lurk in secrecy and shadow.

I see you, demon! Be gone. You no longer serve this being. And they are no longer willing to host you.

Yes.

This much is enough for now. Have hope, dear one. Many cogs are turning in the primordial soup and although your nose is to the grindstone, things are shifting gears in the deep mystery…

*Yes!*

# DEEP-SLEEP RESTORATION

D EAR ONE,

We're pulling out the big guns today to bring focus to "thoughts patterns" that have been jumping all over the place. There has been so much energy coursing through your system, arcing and sparking and firing in all directions. No wonder it's affected your sleep!

Time to ground and soothe. There are two energetic factors to attend to right now.

Firstly, the energy chakra at the back of your neck is currently wide open and wobbling. Its radius blows out into a huge space about four to five feet behind you. It is a portal that you have "opened" to take a look at your history, including painful things that have happened in the past. A "matrix" program was put in place there to create the reality that you experienced, and the interference or static that shows up there is like a background white noise that you have just become accustomed to, so you didn't hear it or see it, until now.

With this reading, Spirit is placing a strategic amethyst crystalline energy structure in the midst of this collage and as a result it sends out a pulse wave that shifts the entire holographic image. The effects are a beautiful, warm, sunny feeling coming into your body from behind you and pulsing through your entire system, so that your aura and energy field outside of your body are radiating and pulsing with a vibrant pattern—life force—yes, you are opening to receive the cosmic life force.

Bathe in that. It is like rich, thick, fertile compost for the soul. It is the Mother. Yes, draw that in like a vacuum…any part of your body that is vibrating with anything other than life force is being saturated with this energy. *Zing!*

You are strong!

Now, you are learning to power yourself from the divine, rather than drawing from your own cells—it is as if you have changed the code in your system to draw power from the Source, whereas it used to be coded differently. Like a car without enough oil, the machinery would get sticky and cause friction. The "old" program had a deviation in the program, so that the normal process of creating energy was short circuiting and creating a feedback loop, depleting and starving the cells. To support this shift, you might consider drinking cell water to assist in the absorption of nutrients and hydrate the cells.

Secondly, a plumb line from the crown of your head extends down into your pelvis. A gentle oscillation on either side is happening, as your spine is being brought into alignment. You can support this change with yoga, massage and or chiropractic care to open the kundalini channel and create that rush and flow of energy through your entire system. And when you sit to meditate, drop your energy through your perineum into the ground beneath you and sink it deep into the earth—it acts as an anchor. You can also then consciously open the *sushumna nadi* up into the crown and open the crown by casting your energy through your crown out into space and through the galaxy and beyond, and allowing the energy coursing through you to pour out of your heart. In the process, you may feel yourself spinning with the planet—quite a sensation.

These practices support the focus of active mental energy toward restoration of deep sleep in preparation for unleashing your creative potential.

Deepest gratitude, and big pat on the back from the world of Spirit. You are doing very, very well. In this moment, you are receiving much encouragement from the Jaguar, who understands well the patterns of chaos, moves without fear in the darkness, and embodies the reclamation of core power.

*Yes!*

# Third Chakra
*Tap Into True Power*

# ACCESSING CONFIDENCE

D EAR ONE,

The first thing brought to my attention is the knot at the pit of your stomach, where the energy is so tightly contracted—think of a vortex that has been spinning so quickly—that it tangles itself up and constricts energy flow to such an extent that it completely thwarts the flow and becomes thick, gnarly and hardened like cement...or like a knotted vine, woody and fibrous.

So this is where the healing is happening now, in your solar plexus, your Manipura chakra, which is all about your personal power and how it relates in the world.

With this chakra knotted, gnarled and tightly constricted, you have been living out of fear. It has felt like your personal power was taken away from you and that you were at the mercy of others and the greater powers that be. Yet what you know deep in your bones is that you have found a way through, by being committed to expanding your awareness and remaining open to learning about the workings of energy and flow. You have come to understand that there is no challenge that can't be worked with consciously and energetically—and the miracle is that it will ripple into the physical world and affect your waking reality, as if by magic.

So I am taking a deep breath and "diving in" to that center of your physical body—to find that there is sticky, black, tar-like gunk here too. It is no wonder you have felt like you are underwater sometimes. As I write these words, the process of unravelling is happening, front and back. *Always* the balance of the energy centers is front and back: the front determines how you present to the world, while the back governs what happens in the unconscious realm. They reflect each other. So to understand the unravelling, imagine a rope that you have twisted and twisted and twisted until it is completely knotted; and as you start to untwist it, it takes a while. You may feel dizzy while this is happening, possibly nauseated too, because we are peering and shining the light into the sticky gunk that has been your modus operandi for a long time, probably since you found your life entwined with a particular being (you know who this is).

There is a lot of fear wrapped up in this dynamic, so you as you are clearing and healing from this, you are restoring balance—restoring justice—to a colossal cultural system that reigns supreme over the country you call home and has even led you to feel uncertain voice standing up for yourself and your rights. It is the David versus Goliath story all over again, and you are right to be in awe of that.

Unraveling, unraveling, unraveling…untwisting and untwisting…

Spirit Guidance would like you to take a moment and see just how perfect the timing of this is—once again—that you would be en route to standing up for yourself at the very moment of this reading.

Divine timing, once again in your favour, is having you walk in with your solar plexus clear, untangled, lit and transmitting the most radiant bright light—so that all of your spiritual power marches into that room and *commands* respect...

There is a popping, sparking sound effect that I only wish I could describe, signaling the unraveling is complete!

Please note: you may be taken onto hands and knees from this. You may hold it together through this process but because of the unraveling and the release, you may be reeling thereafter for a few days. Many knots have been undone and you may also feel "undone" and "unraveled"...

In the next few days, allow yourself to grieve, rage, wail, howl, cry, throw up...whatever needs to expel or be released from your body as you have carried this energy for a long time. As you release it in this way, it may knock you sideways—but know that it is working, that this is part of the clearing, that it is a good thing to feel all these feelings that have been tied up in knots there.

I feel the force of the intimidating rage and the caustic toxicity you have felt directed at you. I invite you to flow compassion and forgiveness back to this being. Remember, we cannot change another person, but we can consciously choose how we react when one throws negativity at you. You have, in the past, absorbed it into your body and let it twist you up in knots. So try it, just try to flow compassion and forgiveness back to them, instead of rage and anger, and you will notice tremendous shifts...in your own ease and peace of mind and also in things that occur in reality.

You are practicing taking the highest road in this way. You are practicing being in alignment with the Higher Power, with this compassion and forgiveness. These qualities are the highest phenomena that a human being can cultivate and experience, as these qualities literally "raise your vibration" and allow you to be free of the tangles and gnarls, the daggers and arrows of negative forces directed at you. It makes you energetically impenetrable...

The compassion comes from a place of awareness, recognizing that this being is miserable and lost in his existence, acting so small-minded that they are unable to 'see' a way clear to a loving and kind place in their heart, really a tragic way of living. And it comes from a place of not knowing. It comes from a place of being so hurt, wounded and confused that they only know how to lash out and leave a trail of destruction in their wake. So understanding this, knowing this (even through your own rage and anger), there is a twinkle of an inkling of a spark of compassion toward them for having a life that is so utterly wretched that they must hurl attacks in your direction.

Yet this compassion detaches you from the reaction and it also helps you to rise above, so you are no longer swimming in the muck at the mercy of attack.

You are becoming your own being. You are becoming independent in your power and you are slowly separating yourself from the cords that bind you to the intensity of attack from others. This is healing, this is you finding yourself. This is finding your way home to yourself and reclaiming your power, reclaiming your consciousness, and reclaiming the thought patterns and emotions that bring you peace and allow you to feel love in your heart. This is self-love. This is powerful.

Shine bright, my friend. Shine so very bright and know that the Universe has your back and your front and your insides out and your upside down. It has you every which way and every configuration of the hot mess and the discombobulated basket case to the radiant triumphant superhero on top of the mountain! You are being lovingly held no matter how you present, no matter how you are in the moment. Knowing this brings such peace, such strength and such courage...

Walk into a room today with your solar plexus supercharged and super powerful. Without their knowing why, the right people will be captivated. What if I am stating the obvious (as you know this in your bones) by saying such things happen and will continue to happen because you are actively working to be in alignment with the Higher Power. You are consciously choosing to surrender to the Highest Good and from this place, anything is possible.

When you surrender to the flow, you tap into the unlimited and infinite potential of the universe. With your conscious intention and your will aligned, miracles happen...

*Yes!*

# STANDING IN YOUR POWER

D EAR ONE,

I was shown a line of energy that hooks through the bottom of your foot (like a tight coil) and then runs through your ankle and all the way up your leg and hip and into your solar plexus, where it flashes like a beacon or a button that is ready to be pressed and triggered. This is a button that gets pressed regularly in relationship (be aware as someone specific pops mind) and continues to activate and aggravate the ankle. Another visual is of the person grabbing you around the ankle while prostrate on the floor, like a last-ditch effort to hang on as you are pulling away. Of course this then triggers a huge amount of emotion in you born of love and compassion.

In a sense, you short-circuit your freedom by having this feedback loop set up. There are heavily armed emotional triggers ready to be pressed and binding you, in your mind, to the other person's needs, even though they are not a particularly needy person, although, as every*body* does, they exhibit emotional needs and a desire to hang on to one they believe can fulfill them.

Another metaphor, of course, is the ball and chain around the ankle. It's interesting that it interferes with your clarity, despite the ways you exercise, practice meditation, and find that spiritual connection in sacred space.

Here is the challenge that Spirit is asking of you: Create that sacred place wherever you are. If you can't make it to your special spot, start with where your feet are. Step out onto the Earth in the morning barefooted and visualize that this trigger button is deactivated. Follow the line with your mind all the way down to that tight coil in your foot, and allow the coil to unravel (picture a screw that tightens in when turned one way; you want to unscrew the energy and allow it to flow into the Earth). This will dissolve and dispel the emotional reactions in you that are hardwired into the relationship.

I see it unravelling clockwise (which is different from a screw's direction) and the energy is kind of like an ice blue. There is a frozen and coldness here, too. Freeing this should flood your mid-section with warmth and a sense of wellness, peace and calm. This is also about standing on your own two feet.

You have been holding a lot in your gut, and you show me a tight fist. This has been your mode of operation for some time while trying to figure things out in your head. So here's a reminder to open to understanding and knowing with your whole body, not just your mind. Let your body be your guide, and your spirit through your body. This way, you will choose the path that is in alignment with your highest purpose.

A "rewiring" is happening in your head, too, as if your nervous system has been jammed and is compressing the bones of your skull.

This may manifest as headaches, or perhaps it shows up as a lot of rumination and stressing.

Moving to your heart, it feels...raw. Yes raw, but oh so radiant. Oh my!

Your spirit is just bursting and shining so bright. Coupled with that strength, it feels like you could take on the whole universe and you are ready to step into that power.

You are showing me that you are ready to raise your vibration, to see the world in a new way, to take off the blinders and be open to the incredible majesty of all that is, with excitement and expectation! There is a giddy excitement at the pure possibility that awaits you in your spirit, and it is bubbling up and ready to overflow into your entire being...and manifest in the life of your creation...

And then there is a pang.

For in the present moment, there is also a deep and stirring sadness in you at the decision you face...and all that "letting go" truly would mean. Your spirit has been weighing up the different visions of your life that are before you to choose...and one way fulfills you in the most profoundly beautiful way at your essence.

And you are asking, "Can I have my cake and eat it too?"

I believe you can.

Others who are ready can grow with you. If your dreams involve another being, ask yourself, is this person willing to grow with me? Maybe your rising vibration is just what the spirit doctor ordered to jolt them into recognizing what they need to do in order to walk alongside one who is claiming their liberation and power...rather than dragging you down by the ankle! (And if this person is someone with whom you no longer relate on the physical plane, then you understand why the separation had to occur.)

Hold the vision of yourself as that radiant magnificent powerful being that you are and then see if a person's energy can match that level of power...if one is willing to shed the layers of energy that hold them rigid in a paradigm of sadness and claim their power, together you would both be a mighty force! Anything is possible.

And if not, remember...you have entered a period of intense transition where you are transforming yourself from the inside out. Discovering the depths of yourself is like finding hidden treasure. Flexing those spiritual muscles is like learning to fly and there can be no stopping you, really. Your spirit is bursting from the seams of your physical form and can no longer be restrained....

You are finding the power to create the very reality of your existence and you can imagine what an ecstatic discovery that is!

Know that you are right on track and couldn't be more so if you tried. Even this process one day you will see is growing, expanding, reconstructing you from the inside out. There is beauty in it, in and of itself, like a child learning to walk and the delight in that mastery; they take little steps, wobbly at first, reaching out for a hand. There are spirits and guides all around you to support you. Speak to them... they are in the animals, in the clouds, in the trees and plants, in the crystals, in the music, in the wind. You are not alone.

Many blessings, dear one, and so much love.

*Yes!*

# SUCCESS WITH FULFILLMENT

D
EAR ONE,

There is a feeling of *wanting* here—wanting a big breakthrough or wanting to kick a goal, getting into gear, engaging, yearning and calling in that feeling of accomplishment and success, and desiring to experience that in your waking world.

In this, there is an important truth to recognize: before you can have that experience in the external world of "reality," a shift must occur within you. You need to feel that accomplishment and success inside of yourself. This necessitates an alignment at your core.

And we feel in you a discord because deep inside of you, you're not even sure you want to be doing what you're doing day to day, and the uncertainty creates an energetic schism.

So there is the *wanting* of accomplishment on this path and yet there is also an internal misalignment of what is true to your core. This is felt in your gut, your solar plexus, like a knot. It feeds into your thought patterns and probably drives you a little crazy.

Know that Spirit is untangling the energetic knot here in your belly, and if over the next week, you could take ten minutes a day to breathe into your belly and focus your attention there, you may find that a lotus flower blooms and opens with a beautiful insight and a realization about the way to move forward. I see the flower opening. The lotus has long been a symbol of awakening and enlightenment—its petals are a beautiful display of sacred geometry and it grows from a seed deep in the mud up through the water (the unconscious mind) to the surface where it blooms for all eyes to see.

It is important for you to know this: it is easy to look for answers outside of yourself and want someone to tell you what to do. The recognition being asked of you here is this:

> *You have all the answers you seek inside of you.*
> *Anything that comes from an external source is not*
> *directly from your center, your heart, your being.*
> *And in this place, you know at your core what it*
> *right for you.*

What brings you the most joy? What inspires you? What exhilarates you? Your homework is to do something that exhilarates you. An activity that takes you WAY out of your comfort zone. This will enliven you, infuse you with vital energy, and get your heart pounding...whether it's a tandem jump from a plane or singing at an open mic night, or maybe it's as simple as going to the gym for an aerobics class.

Imagine yourself having a hobby that inspires and enthralls you. You take that energy into your day job. That passion flows through you on every level, that excitement ripples out to all the people you meet.

The notion of forgiveness is intertwined with this discovery of what truly inspires you. Spirit is asking you to forgive yourself. When is the last time you've made a list and forgiven others?

Now it is time to turn that forgiveness on yourself. Especially in the midst of the heavy slumping sigh that comes at the end of the day, when the mind kicks in wondering why things aren't working out the way you wish.

First things first. Take a moment to acknowledge you are doing the best that you can. You have taken the reins. You are seeking guidance. Ever since you opened the door of self-inquiry and began looking within, you are actively working to make the shift in yourself by showing up to receive. Patience is needed, lessons will be learned in the timing of things that come to pass.

It seems it would be grand if we could snap our fingers and have instant manifestation of all that we desire, but even the novelty of that would wear off. If you got everything you ever wanted the moment you wanted it, you always would be thinking, "now what?"

The cosmic joke is that, in fact, you are getting exactly what you want in every moment. The hardship and the practice of patience and the unraveling over time—there is beauty in that. There are lessons. The fabric of life is woven with threads that you have placed there by your choices. How you are today, will affect who you are tomorrow. Can you see that in every moment we determine how our lives will look tomorrow? Every interaction, every thought, every intention, every action will shape and create how we walk in the world tomorrow.

So how do you choose to be in this moment? What is your contribution to yourself at this time? Do you choose to align with the self-negating thoughts that drag you down and get mired in the delusion of woe? Bringing your thoughts back to the positive takes practice. It doesn't happen over night.

Every time you find yourself thinking thoughts that are detrimental to your empowerment, affirm:

I am love.
I am joyous.
I am successful.
I am free.

Say them slowly in your mind, with space between each word. Charge those words with the feeling of love, the feeling of joy, the feeling of success. At first you will find that they are just words to replace the ramblings of your mind. Repeat them as often as necessary unto infinity. In this way you, "seize the reins of your mind" rather than be at the mercy of thoughts that will carry you like a bolting horse.

Find joy in being an agent. Find the love for working with people. What do you love about it? Focus on the positive. That is the thread that will guide you through. Little things…it doesn't have to be monumental. Maybe it's that you are out and about under the sky. Maybe you get to see lots of houses and how people live. Maybe you learn something from everybody you meet, maybe you smell a beautiful flower.

We know that you are feeling like you wish something would just click into place and have some miraculous door open, but you should know that your spirit is smiling and deep in your essence you can feel the shift, you can feel the change that is happening, like the deepest largest cogs are turning out of sight, but affecting all other smaller cogs up the line.

It is the little things. Like how when it rains, the smell of the sweet Earth is so rich and the plants are rejoicing. It is so simple. What can you rejoice in today? That you are alive?

We are rejoicing because you are alive. We are rejoicing because deep inside of you is the blooming of the lotus. The awakening that happens on the most profound level of existence is activated and reaching up through the muddy, watery depths to reach the sunshine and your spirit is smiling.

So patience, dear one. Before the change is apparent in the waking world, the shifting, turning cogs are being engaged on the inside… and you take the reins by directing your will, your thoughts, your intentions. Remember the recipe:

I am love.
I am joyous.
I am successful.
I am free.

*(Repeat unto infinity and infuse with the charge of those feelings.)*

Bless you.

*Yes!*

# THE MORAL COMPASS

DEAR ONE,

Right now we're speaking to the push and pull on you from being unsettled and not sure where and when you are moving. The word that comes through is *trust.*

Even in your temporary living space, there is deep spiritual work being done. There are cogs turning, there are threads being woven into place that (with your intention) create the fabric of your reality in the year to come. So if you find yourself feeling off center or distracted or out of alignment, the fastest and easiest way to bring yourself back to center is to breathe...*BREATHE*...and tune into your heart with the intention that your heart guides you.

Set the intention that you are ready to receive the guidance that comes from within. The answer will come when it comes. If you are in a place of "I don't know," it is NO.

There is *NO* or *I don't know*...and there is YES.

If it's *NO* or *I don't know*, the answer is NO. Because YES is so blazingly apparent that there can be no doubt or no question. So until you know in your bones without a doubt that the answer is YES, you don't yet have your answer. And sometimes it may take some time to find the YES. So patience is also needed! You don't need to know the answer right away (most of the time)…and if you do need to know right away, then go with your gut instinct. (Did you know that research is discovering that your gut, your gut-brain, is the third source of thoughts?) Your heart is the second and with practice it will become the first.

Let your heart guide you. It will take you on the highest and best possible path. It will lead you to the life of your dreams and bring you more fulfillment and joy than you can possibly imagine….

*Yes!*

# HEALING THE ANCESTRAL LINE

D EAR ONE,

I am called to listen to the deepest meditation track that I have—it is woven with Gamma waves that put the brain into the most powerful trance.

I am also called to tell you again that I love you. And when I say this, it is with all of the God force, divine power that I can muster through this physical form to convey the message from Great Spirit that you are in the tender arms of the beloved and can do no wrong and are held on the waves of love that embrace you.

The struggles, the pain, the discomfort, the despair, mixed with the triumphs, the victories and the delight are all the experience of existence unfolding and the orchestration of the creation game of life. These experiences are why you came. These experiences are what you chose so that you could learn the lessons in the school of the great mystery. These experiences are what you manifest so that you could remember Who You Are.

So through the pain and the despair and the sadness and the intensity of those feelings, allow yourself to witness the joy that is embedded in your spirit—that you are exactly where you are meant to be, everything in your life is appropriate and you couldn't be more on track if you tried. You are doing it! You are living life! You are gaining experience points in the creation game.

Mastery of the Creation Game is being in witness consciousness. That is, watching the show, watching the game, watching the experience while it happens moment to moment through the eyes of the character in the lead role of your movie. Will this movie be a tragedy? A comedy? A romance? An adventure? A fantasy? What if you could decide while you were in the movie playing the lead?

What if paradoxically in this life, you get to be the lead role centre stage in the spotlight, and be the audience sitting front row and centre whilst simultaneously being the director orchestrating the show *in addition to* managing the mechanisms backstage in the rigging, *all at the same time?*

What if mastery of the game was the realizing and awakening that we get to create the game as it unfolds? That the gift and the magic in all of this is that our conscious intention, aligned with free will and surrendered to the Divine, co-creates reality? And when we walk in that alignment, the most incredible magic and synchronicity is bestowed upon us. We walk IN-love. We resonate love. We transmit love. We attract love.

You are probably aware now that you attract devotees and minions by the dozen. This is because you are a veritable powerhouse of Divine Love. This is because you are well-versed in the ancient mystery schools across time and space in multi-dimensions. This is because you have held positions of great spiritual power over the eons.

And here in this life you find yourself so very humbled and so very broken. But that power is not diminished in any way. That power cannot be taken from you. Perhaps this is karma showing you the greatest lesson of all. Your actions affect all lifetimes and all realities throughout all space and time. If you heal in this lifetime, you heal all of your lifetimes. Just as by healing yourself, you affect your entire ancestral line. As you heal yourself, you heal your beautiful mother. She also is no small player in the game of life. There is much wisdom and understanding of the ancient ways in her consciousness—she has just forgotten. Like most souls, we choose to forget when we come in. Part of the joy is finding the pieces of the puzzle and remembering....

As Gangaji once said, "It is like remembering you have a piece of chocolate cake left and you are delighted to find it."

That is the game!!!

And now for the solar plexus and the bile duct that is trembling—trembling and sad with a sense of being "defeated" while the spine is locked. This feels both from the impact of trauma in this lifetime, the fusion with your mother and past-life influences creating the perfect storm....

You show me that with the contraction on your spine, it is pushing you to arch in a certain way that blows out your solar plexus at the front. There is tremendous light bursting out of you here, like you were torn asunder in a past life and there is an opportunity here to autocorrect and gather your light in a way that it is not exploding outwards.

So the guides are unraveling and unlocking the spine at the back so that it can "settle," discharge and balance the energy at your back, so you can regroup and gather your energy that is blasting out of you through the front end. A chiropractor can assist in this process of integration, too.

I am witnessing the unwinding at your back. You can envision this in the next few days too—a counter-clockwise unraveling of the energy at your solar plexus, at your back. Breathe into this unwinding. Allow your spine, the muscles and the nerves to soften and expand and relax. See the energy balancing through this vortex of energy—it moves slowly and gently and it counters the 'tear' at the front.

I feel if you do this in the next few days, it will continue and amplify the impact of this reading and assist you greatly. You feel more relaxed already.

I pray that your mother's spirit is open to healing. I pray that she sees the benefit of clearing her karma and her energy field and her house…and that she too opens the door to the divine, loving Source. Just as with yours, her healing will affect so very many people.

Bless you, dear heart.

*Yes!*

# YOUR TEMPLE IS SOLAR-POWERED

D EAR ONE,

*Thank you for showing up. Thank you for having the courage to soldier on through the most immeasurable suffering.*

These are the words of the Divine Mother coming through me now in this session to come to be with you, tend your wounds and bathe you in the love and light of the divine feminine—the nurturing, soothing healing love of the Goddess embracing all that you are for who you are at your Source. Not for your story or your pain or your suffering but for the spirit that resides within your form, now damaged and broken but alive and more courageous than ever.

Be welcome in this temple of healing, to the love and light that you have yearned to find, not only in this lifetime, but over countless lifetimes of searching and yearning to reconnect. Through such intensity as your current life experience comes the potential of an elevated state of being, where you can find your dignity, find your grace, find your love of yourself, remember that you are the child and the parent and the sibling and the lover and the priest or priestess of the ancient ways, and recall that you are magnificent in all of your glory.

And there are tears that need to be shed, for you have taken on the suffering of humankind in this lifetime. You have absorbed that pain into your body and been at the mercy of so many threads and tangles that wove a web of deceit and lies around you.

And through all of this, even in the darkest depths, there is the innate wisdom in your being that you chose all of it. You signed on for all of it. You as a spirit becoming incarnate chose to take this on because you are such a powerful light. Here in all of this hell and damnation, you can find the light to bring you home and find the courage and the strength to lift you to the surface. This wisdom and intelligence runs rampant in your cells. This is intrinsic in your being—you were born with this instinct and that has been the thread that has kept you alive.

There is great purpose here. There is great and divine orchestration at play. And you have come to the doorstep of surrender where you can push no more and fight no longer—all that is left is to hand your life over to God. And there is great liberation in that. Because with the surrender comes effortless joy. Effortless synchronicity and flow. Miracles happen. Your body becomes the vehicle for the Grace of the divine. No matter how broken or damaged, while you are alive your body houses your divine spirit. And your spirit is powerful beyond measure.

So allow yourself a smile here, because it is like you have just remembered a timeless secret, revealed the greatest treasure, reawakened your spirit, and activated all of the light batteries in your body. Your temple is solar-powered. Soak up the sun every day while you can. Let the sun be your liberation. Feel the breeze on your cheeks.

What if you were in prison—wouldn't your time outside experiencing those two things be the most amazing gift?

It doesn't matter where you are, you can access the elements. Breathe in the light of the golden sun, every day. Fill your lungs with the golden sunlight. Close your eyes and allow the sunlight to filter through your eyelids and into your lungs and into your blood. Feel the light coursing through your veins and into your heart to give you power, give you strength. Fill your heart with this golden light: feel its power, feel its strength, feel the power of the golden sun fill your body with hope, joy and possibility. Let the light shine so brightly within your being that you are lit and this warmth—soak it in.

I see you bathed in the most beautiful golden light.

And this light has the power to knit bones and grow tissue and soothe the soul. And you are orchestrating all of it. Your spirit is guiding this reading—that is the beauty of it. Your spirit shows my spirit where it needs help, what needs to be done, how the knots and tangles can be unraveled, how the patterns of discord can be shifted to return your field to a state of balance. So congratulations are in order here because you have opened the door to remembering. You have opened the door to remembering this intelligence. The intelligence that is your consciousness, your awareness, your connection to the cosmic realms where all there is, is pure potential, pure unadulterated love and grace and raw power.

And through all of your trials and tribulations you have been preparing yourself for this moment. So all that has passed and all that you have experienced is completely and utterly appropriate. Your spirit chose to create those happenings in order to bring you to this moment. Therein lies the cosmic joke. That you would choose such pain and suffering ahead of time to bring you to the crossroads so that you can open the door and see your spirit's radiant magnificence. The hardship and the hurt are the seeds that, when cultivated with compassion, bring the blossoming of the spirit.

Now is the time to be kind to yourself. Now is the time to grieve for all that you have been through. Now is the time to recognize that you are indeed a wise, old soul who has been battered and burdened for so long—and now you can see that you can drop that load like a sack of rocks. You are at choice. And I believe you chose that option because you find yourself here. What are the chances that you are here? It is a miracle in and of itself that you are breathing.

You have not fulfilled your purpose and there is much work to be done! Think of the compassion, the empathy and the deep understanding you now have for anyone who has anyone who has experienced intolerable pain? This compassion knows no bounds. This compassion is intricately linked with the golden light of the sun. This quality or human ability is the highest and most elevated state of being that you can achieve. And you have it in spades. It is saturated in your being. Through all of this and on your road to healing comes wisdom and the ability to lead others out of the darkness, to assist others in the same tangles that you know.

Congratulate yourself, my friend, because you have opened the door. You have opened the door and summoned the power of your own spirit to call you home to yourself, bringing all of the wisdom of the ages across lifetimes of experience to crystallize in your cells and rise from the ashes like the phoenix.

This much, then, is enough for now. Bless you. Bless your body, bless your mind, bless your spirit. Absorb the sunlight!

*Yes!*

# SHIFTING YOUR REALITY

Dear one,

Today I am shown a giant vortex of energy at your solar plexus. There is an imbalance front and back, because the same vortex of energy (or chakra) is minimal at the back. So to see you side on, it is like you are absorbing all of this energy through your midriff to try and counter the lack of motion in the back. It creates a kind of vacuum or sucking energy through your body, nature's way to counter the imbalance.

So one thing to be aware of is it often blows open and then absorbs everything around you. It is good to be mindful of the fact that you unconsciously shut down the energy vortex at the back or plug it up, probably as a survival mechanism to the world you grew up in, or maybe as a result of medication. Unknowingly it created a giant vacuum suck into your body.

So today the spirit guides are gently and scrupulously opening up that energy channel at the back of your solar plexus to balance front and back. Be aware that this act may then bring the light into the things you have shut down over time: there may be memories and feelings that surface as a result, and you may feel out of whack and off center because you are used to functioning with that imbalance. So to have those fields in harmony will feel unfamiliar, and the cathartic clearing that happens a result can be intense and strong. But know that it will pass. Give yourself a few days to come back to center, and this time it will be with more of your personal power zinging. So as you weep and wail and scream into a pillow (a great outlet), you can smile to yourself inside because you know that by doing these things you are clearing and recalibrating. It is kind of like getting a wheel alignment on your car, so the steering wheel doesn't shudder at high speed. You may find in a few days that you are moving through time and space with more ease and that your instinct is once again sharp, your gut channel clear.

Be aware that you can also open and close the aperture of this chakra depending on who you are with or where you find yourself. The hospital for example, would be a good place to reel it in and mute it so that you don't pick up any energetic debris. Airports and shopping malls, or anywhere with lots of humans walking around like zombies and carrying God knows what in their energy fields, are good places to be mindful that you are not absorbing and sucking it all into your system.

Think of your body as an energy transmutation device. You have the natural ability to absorb negative energy, transmute it and recirculate it as light, but the trick is not to hold it in your body or allow it to saturate your field. The key is to connect yourself to the divine Source of all of creation and allow yourself to be the conduit so that everything flows through you into the crown, up through the feet and out through the heart. Add your conscious intention to the mix and you have a powerful transmission. I like the visuals you described earlier. You are literally shifting reality—transforming time and space with your conscious intention. And the fact that you have time to meditate and devote to this healing is really quite beautiful.

From this healing, I see that there are circuits and currents flowing through your body now, like sparks of light pulsing through your cardiovascular system—it is like you are activating and igniting your whole being. And this is easy for you because really this is all information and wisdom that you have accumulated over lifetimes of service.

Stay in meditation. Know I have put an "auto" energy charge in place so that the transmission continues....

Blessings to you, dear heart.

*Yes!*

# Fourth Chakra
*Open the Heart*

# HEART PROTECTION

D EAR ONE,

Straight away I am drawn into the temple of your heart. It is revealing—in curls and furls like a fern frond unfolding, spiraling outwards—how the circumstances you find yourself in are cultivating a deep quality of strength and resilience in you at your core.

The bigger picture of the "why?" and "what for?" is apparent straight out of the gate: why you chose your current experience ahead of time to build and flex this muscle in this way. What you chose this experience for so that you could tap into a place inside of yourself that otherwise may have remained locked away, inaccessible. Perhaps it has remained locked away for eons, lifetimes…and there is an unearthing of an ancient treasure that is happening through all of it, to the point where I am shown in the deep ocean a buried, rusted, covered-in-mollusks key…

Aha! The key to what?!

Only time will tell, but it is a key that you have manifested through all of this...and there is a resounding chuckle in your being at the deeper understanding within you. You get the game, the one that you have played and mastered so many times before.

A pitch, a tone is coming through, like ringing in your ears or the toning of a gong or a bell. It is piercing and growing in volume, and it is accompanied by a pinpoint of light that is expanding...it is the pilot light of your soul, the ignition and spark of your being that has been reduced and condensed and cooked down into a nugget that is packed with nutrient-dense, solidified goodness. It is ready to be watered and activated by pure intention, nourished by will power and focus...and by doing this, you unlock and enrich all of your gifts, ALL of your gifts...

Wow! Are you ready for this? You thought you were a powerful manifestor before...and now you are opening the palm of your hand. There is a shimmering, sparkling golden sphere before your eyes, visible for anybody to see, indicating that you are literally remembering how to work energy to manifest in reality *in real time...*

\* \* \*

And now you are showing me the disjointed, jostled, hammered part of your heart that has taken so very many hits over the years. It is like an iron sword that has been forged in the fire and hammered over and over again to be shaped and formed by the smith to create a most beautiful instrument of power. The sword represents the divine masculine...

And as I write this letter to you, the most beautiful song of devotion to the divine comes on the shuffled play list: It is called "Bhagavad Gita Shlokas" by Yogeshwara and Suresh from the album *Ayur Veda.*

Look it up online and listen. Next, listen to the song "Eyes Wide Open" by Tony Anderson. Both are pertinent to the healing that will continue over the next three days.

\* \* \*

If at all possible, keep away from negative influence for three days. This is energetic heart surgery of the most intricate and delicate kind, so if you are to encounter the intense furnace of a rage-filled person, consciously shield yourself first and then surround yourself in the violet flame of St. Germaine. Violet represents the highest vibration on the spectrum discernible by human eye. In you, around you, and through you, call on St. Germaine and Archangel Michael, the angel with the sword of protection.

Another ancient piece of wisdom to supplement the visual is to inhale the scent of black pepper before you talk or meet the person and see a whirlwind of energy around you that no external force can penetrate without your permission.[1] There are many powerful plant medicines. You are being shielded now with state-of-the-art, advanced civilization celestial technology, an impenetrable force field shield— around your form, your etheric body and your energy field—about twenty feet wide so that you can deeply rest in this space, in this cocoon of golden threads like an egg, lying on a cloud of fluff and cotton wool to nurse and nourish your being in this sanctuary of softness, to counter and dissolve the impact of any assault.

I'll say it bluntly: recognize that indeed you have been in the line of fire and that your body trembles with the reverberation of violation

---

1 From Scott Cunningham's *Encyclopedia of Magical Herbs.*

and assault. And with this recognition comes the flood of tears that want to be expressed and released: sob, wail, cry, let it flow, baby. I hear a lullaby…'tis the Divine Mother now here and enfolding you in the arms of the Goddess…holding you, supporting you, tending to you, carrying you. Allow yourself to be the little child for a few days, and just really tune into the little one's needs and give all love you can, whether it's a hot bath or chocolate or a teddy bear or meditation in a beautiful place, maybe mineral springs, the ocean, a deep tissue massage, a hearty, warming meal—wherever you find sustenance for your being. Please gift yourself this while you navigate the maelstrom, for you have not found safe harbor quite yet and your ship is a long way from shore…

May the long time sun
Shine upon you,
All love surround you,
And the pure light within you
Guide your way on…

These words have been woven into a beautiful song by Snatum Kaur (original words by Mike Heron) that I'm listening to as I write.

Envision your ship steering into port, into safe harbor where you may rest and you may replenish your supplies and you may drop anchor to restore the vessel.

And as I write these words, hummingbird medicine is here: the magical nature spirit that soothes and neutralizes the vibration of violence. If you find yourself trembling, shaking, your body is seeking to release that—so let yourself shake, dance or vibrate that out of you. Trauma release exercises are good, too.

All of these things will replenish you and restore you and water the nugget of goodness that is condensed within you. You are quite the light warrior, and all of the experiences you have journeyed are fuel for your own fire, the fire that is ready to once again shine so very brightly.

What the future holds, only time will tell—but know that by anchoring your spirit in your body and accessing your light, the guidance will come through loud and clear in your body as to which is the pathway forward. It will be plain as day. All illusion and threads and webs of confusion are hereby banished and cleared in a puff of smoke *kapoof!*

Rest deeply. Rest long. Rest...

And tomorrow you will awaken as if from a dream, to see clearly in the mirror, who you are in all your glory and magnificence...

You will remember Who You Are.
You will remember Why You Are.
You will remember What You Are.

You are the master of your own destiny. You are the master of your reality, and with that mastery you recognize that you are also in total surrender to the divine. 'Tis the cosmic joke—*huzzah!*

It is done.

*Yes!*

# WRITE TO YOUR HEART

D EAR ONE,

There is a feeling that you are looking for something to hold on to, that you are grasping at thin air. This is symbolic of your mind and character looking for an old default setting that has recently been changed in your world. This shift is creating a little short circuit in your energy field, as you look to the old familiar "routine." You are realizing again and again, "Oh yeah, things are different now" and it hurts each time you trip over that wire. Your Spirit is asking you to *fully feel it* in your bones and through your whole paradigm, so that you don't have to experience that knee-jerk response each time you have that realization.

This is part of your integration and learning to play in this dimension. Little nuggets and homework for you to practice flexing your expanded-perception muscles!

Oh my, this is big.

This is very, very big.

And this reading is part of it—all the letters and words are part of the "story" of you coming home to yourself through the grand magnificent orchestration of recent events. Let that percolate!

Spirit says, "Ha, ha! Now watch your dreams for affirmation."

And again, look to the play of light. Notice if your fingers and hands are tingling in the next few days. Don't mistake it for symptoms, but think of it as energy kicking in and about to get activated, big time!

Your thoughts are being linked through the top of your crown chakra, to your heart, to your hands—a conduit of Cosmic consciousness.

Please start writing.

Whatever, whenever, about whatever is kicking around in your head, even if it is, "WTF am I doing? I don't know what to write... I need to check on the potatoes boiling." Writing will activate a trickle that is waiting to come through, that will turn into a stream, that will turn into a current, that will turn into a torrent, that will join with other rivers and merge through the rapids, that will turn into a cascade, that will flow and take you to the ocean.[2]

Yes, others will be picked up in the expression and the sharing of yourself in the waves that, in turn, open them to the possibility and expansion that you are being asked to hold. Which is only the journey of the soul into its highest evolution and most magnificent expression of itself, that's all. "Just playing small, don't mind me"...no chance.

Yeah! Can't wait to read it.

Now, don't forget to pat yourself on the back and congratulate yourself occasionally. You are creating yourself anew every day, a

---

2    The ocean is a Jungian symbol of the subconscious; and other lines of thinking, it represents a unity consciousness.

cosmic task that requires discipline and trust and surrender in the most major way.

Just know that you are fully equipped to handle anything that comes your way. You got a good hand of cards this time around. There is support for you wherever you turn. It's almost like you are being lifted up and held by your loved ones and those unseen in such a way that you can easily reach up and grab the torch. Yes, a torch like the flaming brand in the Olympics or the one that Statue of Liberty holds aloft. I see you holding it high overhead. Ah, it is a beacon....you are a beacon for others to see the light. *Ooooh.* Breathe that in next time you are alone in nature. Go ahead and hold that posture. It will feel like a perfect fit...like you are stepping into a perfectly designed outfit to fit your form and it is snug and it feels good. And, dang, do you look good! And you can know that inside and out because I suspect you are going to be the focus of quite a bit of attention in days to come.

OK, back to Earth, here and now in this moment. There is still the fragility, the rawness, the tenderness....like a wound that is slowly healing and still tender to the touch. But you can see that it is healing. You know your progress is on track, and the wound is healthy and pink and regenerating nicely. It doesn't even appear to be deep anymore. It is surface and superficial, and not interfering with your functioning.

Looking at it, you know that you will have a nice scar there for the rest of your days as a reminder, but it will no longer hurt you as it did. Even the scar doesn't seem like it is a bother; rather it acts as a reminder of the lessons you are learning through all of it.

There is a beautiful, playful creative energy around you. See if you can tune into it each night before you go to bed. It starts as a spiral at the front and back of your heart and morphs and moves around your head, bringing ideas and inspiration. If you get any bright ideas in the next wee while, pay attention. There is strong stuff here, and a sound that accompanies it. Listen. Tune into it and enhance it that way...

* * *

And yet there is also a feeling of potential and trepidation, as you stand in a place of "Now what?"

Remember all of this emotion is contrast, fine-tuning you to "feel" the presence of love that is here for you now, so that it's not just an intellectual understanding but a full somatic body experience...yes... you are radical and awesome and courageous and amazing!

Know that, in your bones, beyond the ego...

*Yes!*

# RELEASING THE FAMILY CORDS THAT BIND YOU

D EAR ONE,

In this moment, the energy is slow to start moving. Whether it is because your system is in shock or the whole planet is in shock—this remains to be seen.

It is almost as if you have had a wet blanket thrown across you in an attempt to stifle and dampen the flame within you.

The impact and the jolt that is running through the light grid and network of consciousness is akin to an energy surge that temporarily knocks out the power and takes out the electricity. Only this energy surge is not just one house or even one town or a city, it is planetary wide—and anybody who is sensitive to energy or doing the good work of liberating their consciousness is particularly affected by this surge.

Once again the blessing in all of this is that you manifest a situation that was troublesome and a little painful, but very quickly you also manifest the tools and the means to analyze it and understand the larger implications. So in this way, you are also being the conduit and allowing the planetary energy to flow through you and to catalyze in your form in such a way that you can examine it and use it to serve the highest good.

Thank you, hands! Thank you, knees! Thank you, body! For taking a hit so a "jolt" could be felt through the system—so these words would be written and this clarity and insight gained. Let's just say a little prayer that all future lessons come and are gleaned with no harm done to the physical body and no disruptive forces are needed to get the message through. We might say the same prayer for Mother Earth, that no harm be done to her in the lessons that humanity must surely learn in order to walk in balance and be connected to Great Spirit.

Within the contraction in your middle back, there is a vortex of energy here swirling and lit up, charged and activated, even agitated. The energy of some inflammation is present here. If you can get a massage in the next few days, that would be beneficial. At your mere reading of these words, energy is travelling up into your neck, creating a deep relaxation and preparing you for a restful sleep needed to "recover" from the high tension of the last few days.

When faced with an emergency, the body functions on adrenals and nervous tension to deal with the situation. For you, it has become necessary to blow off some steam and decompress in your body, to allow turning of the gauge that cranked up to red alert back down to green. Hot soups and hearty meals will help also. Eat well, nourish your body with foods that taste good and enrich and warm your system. Whatever it is that has been weighing on your mind, just know you did the right thing and you are to be commended for your response . . . ability as well as your actions.

A member of your family who has been with you travels with a kind of mechanism that creates a short circuit in the human energy field. If life was a science-fiction movie (which it actually kinda is), imagine a soft of spherical device that flies alongside them and sends out a pulse wave that momentarily disrupts and distorts the bio-energetic field. This person is not aware that this is with them—it generally presents in the personality or character as someone who is demanding and needy for attention. Placed there when they were small, it has served as a kind of a defensive survival mechanism used to manipulate situations and bend people to their will.

Fortunately you can disarm such a device, which functions on an almost undetectable frequency, just being aware that it is there. Another blessing in all of this is the honing of that awareness. It may sound like fantasy—"yesterday I saw and pulled off an alien clawed hook device from someone's back"—but this is how the energy presents and in the unseen realms anything goes. Whether science fiction, fantasy or mythology, we are talking anything is possible in the realms of consciousness where imagination has no boundaries, and usually is.

As you become aware of such influences, you can also recognize that you do not need to be at their mercy: you can dismiss, dissolve, remove, banish, disintegrate, unravel (the list is endless) the energy that is affecting your physical body. Part of this is tuning your awareness to this level of the game, this level of the playing field. Unless you live in a sanctified bubble, there are mechanisms that you can navigate and avoid or consciously free yourself from, if they have affected your field.

Most people exist like they are sleepwalking (maybe they have a little insight and think that means they are enlightened) and carry around a host of creepy crawlies or methods and devices put in place at a tender age as survival mechanisms. These were the tools they needed at the time to survive their reality. Everybody is doing the best that they can but most people don't realize they walk around with these constructs of reality embedded in their "program."

Enough sci-fi for now. Suffice to say, you are a student of the great mystery and absorbing a lot of lessons very quickly. Take care of you—you have been navigating quite the energetic mine field.

And cleanse your house! Burn frankincense, copal, rose—infuse this smoke into all the nooks and crannies with the conscious intention to reboot and reset the energy of your house to suit and match your vibration.

This will also weave that desired shield of protection in your space. Mirrors and doors, place your magic touch on them—envision your force field there and weave it around your loved ones, too.

*Yes!*

# CLEARING TRAUMA IMPRINTS

A LOHA, BEAUTIFUL ONE,
Thank you for taking the time to give this to yourself . . .

It is time to heal a past traumatic event that caused a jolt in your system. Consider the first distressing event that comes to mind when reading these words. I know this event left you sad in some way, yet pat yourself on the back for a moment to acknowledge how you responded in the moment with grace and dignity, even though under a shocking situation.

This whole experience was about you being "jolted" out of your habitual thought patterns and now you are ready for a heart expansion that has you embracing the world in a new way.

Whether or not you are religious in the Christian sense, the energy of Jesus Christ is present, placing an energetic hand on your heart. Jesus Christ is really a symbol of the Christ consciousness within all of us—that compassion, kindness and healing that we all yearn to know and live.

And now the focus shifts to your feet, to *ground, ground, ground.* Life energy just wants to flood your whole system in a beautiful, balanced way. Just imagine that you manifested this whole experience so that you would enable yourself as a vessel to "hold" and contain more energy . . . and bring it through, especially that beautiful heart energy that is now pulsing and vibrating right out of your chest.

Take care to eat root vegetables to help ground—carrots, squash, potatoes, pumpkin, beets—and as you eat these, feel your feet sending down tendrils and roots into the earth to connect with her.

And if you find yourself teary and a little unraveled from all of this, it is part of the clearing. Imagine it like you are vibrating out the old form and allowing the new form to be. It is as if you've had a redesign from the inside out so that you can access more of your truth and power! From this all good, powerful infusion, you may be feeling "larger than life."

*Yes!*

**4 - 5**

# Strengthening the Heart

D EAR ONE,
I see you, I feel your pain…I hold your heart in my awareness with love.

These words that come through me and onto this page are for you to absorb and read again and again to receive the transmission of energy that flows through them.

You are on notice from Spirit. It is official—that the time has come. All that you have been and all you have experienced and all that you have put forth into the world—now is the time to harvest from that experience and all that you have been cultivating.

Your heart is radiant. Your light shines so brightly and the ailments you suffer are simply a misalignment of your body/mind/spirit to your highest purpose.

Entertain the idea that you—in your highest, most joyful expression—have so much love and kindness to share, and the ways that this can come through you are infinite.

Play with the energy of love. Does it come through your heart today in purple spirals with fireworks? Does it come through you today as the written word? Does it come through you as words you speak? Does it come through you as action you take to help a child?

You are an exceptionally sensitive person, sensitive to reality. And perhaps over the years, it felt like everybody wanted a piece of you and little by little it chipped away at your sense of self. People are attracted to your bright shiny light and it seems everybody wants to take a little piece of your energy, thinking that in doing so it will fulfill some aspect of themselves. And yet you know from your experience now that it is not possible, that they must find the light within.

The beauty of it all is that there are worlds within worlds within worlds for you to explore. The vast and infinite aspect of your being that is divine—this is your spirit and here anything is possible. In this place of cosmic intelligence, there is infinite potential. So now that we have opened up the parameters of the creation game and tapped into the realms of holy communion, allow yourself to align with these words, the we being you and I, as the channel of this prayer:

We pray together for your healing, for the liberation of your spirit for the          restoration of balance in your physical body for the fulfillment of your highest   purpose and the clarity of your mind. We pray for the alignment of your   body/mind/spirit and that that these aspects of your being are synchronized and   zinging with harmony. This is your portal for joy and happiness. This is your release from suffering.

Remember that there is a distinction between pain and suffering, as acknowledged by His Holiness the Dalai Lama—there *can* be one without the other. You might be in the most incredible pain, but you may not be suffering. I have witnessed this in my father over a lifetime of intolerable pain. I have journeyed this experience myself with the most acute and chronic sensations. When we detach the "story" or the ego mind from the picture, there is liberation.

So much of your present opportunity is to deconstruct the idea of who you thought you were and what you represented in the world. To be open to the possibility that you are now embarked upon a journey of recreating yourself and manifesting a form that is in alignment with your highest purpose. Let the healing work be the deconstruction and the recreation. The phoenix in the fire, born from the ashes.

Muse on this concept for a moment: that you as a spirit chose this experience before you came in. You knew that it would give you the opportunity to evolve and grow as a spirit....

Now I am directed to extract a dark energy from your field. It feels suffocating, particularly around your neck. This energy has been entwined through the major organ that is your heart, and crosses your thymus gland and your lungs and chest.

I banish this form, I banish this entity that no longer serves you. Part of this healing is bringing your awareness to the forces that occupy your physical body. Awareness is key. When we are in an emotionally fragile state, we are particularly vulnerable to open the door for unwanted forces. Awareness is key. Who occupies your body? Use your free will to cast out any "qualities" of your character that don't fit anymore. You are changing costume. What costume would you like to wear for this next scene. What suit would you like to house your spirit?

The lower density vibration emotions are breeding grounds for negative forces. They are quagmires and cesspits where energy forms of questionable integrity lurk. So what emotions plague you? Are you resentful? Are you fearful? Are you sad?

Emotions travel in waves and when they flow through you and

are expressed, you are able to release them and grow. If stifled, they create a backwash and fry the circuitry of your nervous system. We are simple creatures, really, gifted with an extraordinary sensory apparatus, but we have lost the wisdom of the elders and the indigenous knowing that Great Spirit will provide when we live in service and surrendered to the highest good.

I ask you to surrender here and now. Surrender your well-being and your spirit and your body and your mind into the hands of Creator. That we pray together for a miracle for your body (and cash in on those merit points earned)! And I pray that you are guided to know deep in your core what is right for you. And I pray that the guidance from your heart is loud and clear enough for you to know the way forward. To know deep in your bones what action to take. And I hold the vision of you healed and joyful and free of pain and suffering—I hold this vision in my heart and in my mind's eye—that you are fulfilled in your purpose, living in gratitude and in sync with all of creation, so that you too may experience the bliss of a life in devotion and overflowing with love.

Yes. This much, then, is enough for now.

*Yes!*

## 4 · 6

# Nourish and Nurture Your Soul

DEAR ONE,

When I tune into you, I see the image of a lotus flower opening and sparkles emerging out of the blossom. This is always symbolic of the flowering of the spirit—the opening of the mind and the evolution of consciousness within a being.

It is time!

And it is testimony to the fact that you have put the hours in to nourish yourself and train your focus. By aligning your intention to heal, you open to receive and thus surrender to the Divine plan . . .

Huzzah!

With this we acknowledge a badge of honor earned here—a marker in time, a celebratory infusion of goodness coming your way to receive the rewards of merit that you most truly deserve!

This insignia gifted to you by Spirit—it is the empowerment and clarity bestowed upon you to claim sovereignty over your life, your experience, your environment and your home.

You are claiming your power. You are tending to your needs. You have become aware of sticky threads in your experience and you can see the way clear to disentangling yourself from them. Your healing will amplify with this realization, for you have transcended the past, in which you faced the steady gaze of disbelief directed at you from others who didn't have the bandwidth to understand what you are up to!

Sigh, yes . . . I see you taking a deep sighing breath, as if your whole body relaxes after being held rigid and guarded for some time, just at the thought!

*Ahhhhhhhhhh.*

Deep at your core there is a tension that is releasing now. You may fall asleep, because the guides are unraveling the energy that extends the length of your body and woven through your spinal cord and nervous system. Allow yourself to rest as needed in the next few days. This is a tightly coiled spring that is releasing and there is much energy that has been held in place for some time.

Sigh . . . more deep sighs . . . sighs of relief . . .

If you need to sigh often in the coming days and release a sound effect with the sigh—by all means—that will assist in the somatic release. Get as vocal as necessary! Yawning is good too—it is the same thing in a different form. Know that you have the support of the entire universe (and that's no small thing) to do whatever you need to do to take care of yourself.

Ah, it's good to know the entire force of the universe has got your back.

Yes . . . the glittering, sparkling, vortex of stars is drawing me down, down, down, down, down into the depths that have no end and to the zero point . . . the void . . . the pregnant moment . . . pure potential . . .

The universe loves you. I love you. I am so filled to the brim with love for who you are and all that you be.

If it were ever possible to burst from love, I think I just might . . .

Yes, all this travelling to you across the heart waves . . . and the pressure being released from the back of your neck and head, so that your spine may come into alignment. Feel the energy being drawn out of your arm, allowed to flow . . .

*Yes!*

## 4 - 7

# DEEP HEART HEALING

D EAR ONE,

The first thing that reveals itself is a feeling that your spirit does not know which way to turn. That it finds itself doing U-turns, backtracking in a perpetual pattern of trying to find the way forward and feeling like it is being turned around.

And this feels directly related to your heart. While there is much joy in you to be expressed, there is a sense of resignation in your heart that is wondering how to stop bumping up against the walls that have you pinging around like a pinball.

I feel sadness related to that. That there is a deep yearning for clarity and a shining light on the path of least resistance, the way forward.

So the guides are here today and they are unraveling the corkscrew energy that has your heart vortex contracted in "survival" mode. And there is a word that comes with that and it is "unleash"...that you are here today unleashing your heart power and unleashing your vital energy force so that it may flow into all of your cells—your bones, your tissues, your nerves, your blood and your lymph. All of your body's systems have been on "lock down," so to speak, while your mind has been grappling with your current perceived state of imbalance.

When people believe their state of health to be imbalanced, there is often a tidal wave of fear that washes over them and creates a kind of rigidity in their mindset. They feel at the mercy of doctors, hospitals and/or other "experts" working within a system that is doing its best to heal you the only way they know how.

So I am going to ask you to open your mind just a little—so that the door can swing ajar and you can feel the flood of light that we are bringing to you here today.

This is healing in a way that is far beyond the reach of Western medicine…the energy we are shifting is not measurable on any scan or test at this moment in time. Your experience is the testimony—how you feel and how your body responds to the light that is pouring into your body now.

And with this opening, it is creating a space in you and a receptivity, and perhaps a shift in your perceptions about the reality of the Great Mystery. Spirit always has a way of affirming the work with a situation or sign that leaves no doubt that this is real. So there may indeed be a coincidence that you experience in the next few days that will bring that affirmation. Perhaps a vision will come in meditation that will manifest into being, or perhaps a memory will surface, releasing a tangle of the past.

From here, I am taken to your throat.

There is a feeling of hands around your throat. It's not clear if this is actual or energetic, but there is a tumbling of words and feelings that want to pour out of you from your throat. This seems to affect the back of your neck too—do you ever experience it as a stiff neck? We are clearing that from your field.

A piece of music comes on as I write, "Eyes Wide Open" by Tony Anderson.

It is pertinent to our work here, as it is paving the way for you to see the energy field and the "pool" that you are swimming in. Together today, we are bringing the light into the shadow areas of your life that have been creating discord and disease from the unconscious realm. It is healing you from the inside out. Healing you from behind the veil.

Together we are examining your field of consciousness to shine the light into the areas where there is the vibration of energy that is unresolved and unhealed. It is powerful work and it takes courage to open to that and for that I am grateful for your showing up and being ready to take the deep dive.

Again I am taken to your heart and I am shown a sort of metallic contraption in the heart field, symbolic of one who has had to armor themselves and put defense mechanisms in place. I am only ever shown something if it is there to be cleared and the person is ready to experience the shift that follows. So there may be an outpouring of emotion that comes with this. There may be a softening in your heart where you feel deeply.

It is important to allow any grief or sadness or anger to surface in the next few days—and really nurture yourself, if that is the case. Put yourself first and give yourself time to really feel it and allow it to move through you and out of you in the wave that carries emotions.

With that clearing comes a clarity in your mind, like the lights have just come on in a new way that allows you to see the world through different lenses. It affects your whole state of being.

Let's take a moment to congratulate you for the amount of energy you have shifted already in this reading and acknowledge you for having the courage to receive this.

\* \* \*

As with any person I work with, I say, "take what resonates, leave what doesn't fit." Some of it may sound like gobbledygook and woo— any yes it is absolutely both of those things. The validation that this is real is your experience throughout and to follow.

Let the words of this reading be a support as the mind tries to comprehend what on Earth just happened. In truth, it is beyond anything that the mind can grasp…it is a healing direct from the Great Mystery.

There are no words or rationale that can put it in a box or categorize it. I merely ask that you remain open to possibility and allow yourself to feel what you need to feel, knowing that my intention is absolutely aligned to your well-being and your healing and wholeness.

And with that, I pray that you find the light within you. That the way forward is direct and clear, unhindered by your life circumstances.

That your path to healing and fulfillment is shining bright for you to see. That the guidance from your heart is loud and clear, and that you receive the support you need emotionally, physically, spiritually and mentally to heal.

Yes, this much then is enough for now.


*Yes!*

# FIFTH CHAKRA
*Express Truth*

# A Fine-Tuning of the Higher Chakras

D EAR ONE,

"*Zing*" is the first word that comes through.

The act of reading these words is generating your *zing!*

It begins with an unraveling of the energy at the front and back of your neck, creating spaciousness in there.

Humming, singing, speaking, laughing, yelling and poetry are all things that wish to come forth through your throat chakra. And today you are also receiving a "crown chakra activation," which is basically opening a portal to the realm of spirit and higher awareness, so pay attention to your dreams! There should be some potent messages coming to you as guidance and "next steps."

A fine tuning is occurring the bones in your skull: think of energy vortexes coming out of each ear and then follow the line of each vortex until it goes through the bones of your skull and deep into your pineal gland where the vortexes meet; this is a gland that with age becomes calcified. In a young child, the pineal gland is soft and spongy; you've seen that look of wonder and awe in their eyes as they explore the world around them…even something so simple as water. That gland is what we are "softening" and opening too. So that you see the world through the eyes of a child, with the wisdom of your years and being open to the infinite realm of spirit…

It's like you've put your hand up in Cosmic School and want to learn, learn, learn what there is to learn about the great mystery, the Divine, the Beloved.

And with this tuning comes a heart expansion, a heart-opening experience and my prayer is that you have another phenomenal experience so there can be no doubt in you of a greater power at work and your place in the scheme of things.

The word "trust" arises and I know that you do, but it is a reminder to know that after the storm comes the most beautiful clarity and golden light, with that zing of excitement too. It's like the excitement a woman experiences before the birth of a child: she is tired of carrying that weight, but rests knowing that any day now there is going to be this whole, life-changing glorious experience.

Whether recently or for a long time, you've tended to carry another's heaviness on your shoulders, bearing it like a sack of bricks, taking on the energetic overflow. With the weight bearing, energetic flow can get blocked and travel up into your neck, and then you're walk around feeling like your head is separate from your body and it disconnects you from your heart. For this, yoga is good. Massage is good. Acupuncture is good. The expense is an investment in your smooth transition to a bigger-picture vision.

You are being asked to expand your consciousness out, to get bigger—not physically but energetically—so that you can be lighter. More power. More energy.

And with that, lightning bolts come out of your fingertips… everything you touch becomes charged and statically ignited. It is essential to be centered when you are wielding that much power, otherwise fuses connect in ways that arc and spark and create flames!

Breathe into your heart and tell yourself it's going to be OK. Any yoga poses or back bends that open the heart would be beneficial too. If you give yourself some time each day, you could see that you generate this beautiful golden white light in your heart…take some time to build it, generate it, feel it, watch it extend out.…

It is important that in the next few weeks you keep your energy "pure" from negative influence as much as possible because, being so open, you are like a dumping ground for stress even if it is not consciously directed at you. You tend to take on the overflow. You are like an energetic anchor: if you are off center, it tips the whole boat and then you are in for a rocky ride.

And now I see that you are showering in this beautiful aquamarine energy, like tropical water. It is invigorating you and your body is thirsty for this color. It is angelic and celestial and earthly all at the same time, and it is filling you up to overflowing so that you don't feel drained and depleted, so that you are at the top of your game and able to hold that anchor effortlessly, even through the storm.

And spirit is bathing you in sparkly stars. So that when you look out at the world, you are looking at everything through sparkly eyes.

Yes, Spirit is taking you to that place of stillness…absolute stillness so that all there is, is pure reverberation of source.

*Yes!*

**5 - 2**

# Reclaim Your Consciousness

EAR ONE,

Right now the energy is thick and fast, bubbling out with great power. It is a clearing of old karma—not just in this lifetime, but across multiple lifetimes. By having this clearing, it is making available to you, the infinite pool of energy from the source, tuning you into the vibration of Creator, the All that is, the ultimate OM, the source of all life.

And it is *so ready* to flow through you that it started to bubble up and burst out of you . . . onto the page through these words. With this connection to Source, comes the ability to manifest—BIG time.

So be mindful of what thoughts you are broadcasting, because they are indeed calling in what you are creating in the waking world. And if you fall back into old habits or the default negative, to which we are especially susceptible when in an emotionally jolting situation, then you will manifest more of the old tedium that you have now worked so hard to free yourself of.

What a concept! Being receptive, showing up to read these words and receive an infusion of positive energy is work, *the work*, the best kind of work there can be. It is devotion, to yourself, to your well-being, to your spirit. The rewards will come to those who do the work.

Even if that reward is just simply happiness or contentment or peace, for no good reason.

I am love.

I am joyous.

I am successful.

I am free.

If you do find yourself weathering a storm—and it's not a matter of if, it's a matter of when because that is the nature of life, that is when your mind spins like a wild compass. That is when it is important to remember your mantra, to ground you into the positive stream rather than let your ship get steered off course and be buffeted by the wind and waves . . . or worse yet, be washed up on the rocks.

All storms, all challenges, all obstacles are lessons in disguise and by coming through the storms, we grow, our characters are strengthened, and our resilience and fortitude is solidified.

In the words of Master Charles Cannon, "the tests will come" . . . and indeed they do. Because every time we come to a crossroad, we must make a choice.

The intention here is this: with the work you have been doing, you now have the grounding, the insight, the strength and the intuition to follow the path that resonates with your heart in the grandest sense of the word. If you can't hear your heart's messages, find the place of stillness first. Find the place of deep inner calm. Visualize the most perfectly still lake, with a mirror surface, reflected the sky above. With absolute stillness comes absolute clarity, a knowingness so strong and so complete that there can be no doubt.

And you have been practicing dropping into stillness as of late. Even if it seems difficult and your mind runs wild, there are times when you notice that you are completely present to the here and now . . . that is, All It Is . . . pure unadulterated presence of mind, stillness, creation coursing through your veins as light and love and power. And it may be that you find yourself drifting off. Do you fall asleep? Or are you simply in the deepest meditative state that you have known? The former is slipping into the unconscious, the latter is charged with awareness.

I am love.
I am joyous.
I am successful.
I am free.

Really this time together has been a fine-tuning of your focus, an attunement of your awareness, and a sharpening of your senses to expand the bandwidth of your perception. This is meaty stuff, far more impactful than a reality TV show downed with a greasy burger and a couple of beers, or variation thereof (the "go to" of most of the human race to tune out).

So congratulations again, and kudos from the spirit realm, which is applauding your commitment and devotion to the awakening of the Self. If life were a video game, your "merit bank" or "experience points" have now had a nice fat chunk deposited in its cache.

Just know that there can be a time of resting on your laurels, knowing that like a stone thrown into that lake, the ripples will reach far and wide, and eventually reach the farthest shore. And it is good and appropriate to take stock, reassess and see where you are at and contemplate your navel . . .

But there will also come a time for action. Movement. Engagement. And you will know when. Remember to hold the thought and intend:

*The waves of flow come back to me threefold.*
*It is effortless and easy*
*and I respond with grace and integrity.*

Pray for that, align with that, talk to Creator about that . . . know you are able to handle the volume of energy that is coming your way, and you can remain in balance, in your center, in your place of stillness, in your place of gratitude and joy.

Take time each day to find your happy place . . .

Where is it in you? Is it in your body? Is it in your mind? Is it in your heart? Is it a place you've visited? Is it a feeling? Is it a friend? Is it a pet? Is it your bed? Is it a piece of music? Maybe it is all of the above.

Layer upon layer, this work has cleared the debris out of your energy field so that now you are ready to receive this beautiful cosmic activation . . . I see you sitting in contemplation, cross-legged, in the middle of a sacred geometry structure, surrounded by the universe with the most exquisite light emitting from deep within. This "imprint" of this image is like an emblem or an official seal from the universe, kind of like a badge of honor, recognizable by other beings of like mind (and from the unseen world and other nations way beyond just the crazy two legged ones).

It is a symbol of attainment. An award, if you like, for the effort on your part to dismantle and reconstruct yourself from within. For due diligence and devotion to liberation of your spirit.

So sit with that and know that there is always more . . . it's never ending. There is no goal. You are exactly where you are meant to be, right here and now in this moment . . . and everything that is happening is perfection. It is what it is.

Congratulate yourself for showing up, because that is really all that is required . . .

Then carry that out into your waking world. Show up for your work. Show up for your clients. Show up for your old cars. Show up for your home space. Be present, be fully present whatever you do—bring ALL of your focus and attention to whatever it is you are doing, whether its washing dishes or having a hair cut or perfecting your stage performance or designing the latest gizmo that will save the planet. You can even show up when you are eating a meal or having a pee. Be fully conscious, be fully present, be fully aware . . . be here now.

Hawk medicine has been with us through this reading, chiming in through the windows of the temple, the Messenger . . .

Go forth and prosper, dear one. You have earned your badge of honor, and while you may feel like a new babe, this life game never stops in revealing Who We Are to ourselves. The hard times are the lessons, the good times are the rewards . . .

Sending you so much love and gratitude for the willingness to look and see how magnificent you are. (And on cue the sun comes out from behind a cloud and blasts through the window sending rainbows around the room through the crystal ball.)

Affirmation. Yes. Validation. Yes. Recognition. Yes.

Welcome to the new you.

*Yes!*

# ENTITY EXTRACTION

D EAR ONE,
I trust that these words will reach you eventually as I take a deep breath filling the lungs with the oxygen-infused life force, breathing deeply *along with you* as we call this into your body, your mind, your spirit…

This infusion of healing energy that is now entering your lungs and your body, while you rest in a state of receptivity, starts to circulate through your blood, into your heart, up into your brain where it ignites and activates your consciousness.

Your eyes begin opening wide at the sensation and laughter escaping your lips. On a very deep and profound level, you get the cosmic joke. You get the irony of where you find yourself. You get the hilarity of the fact that you are this exquisitely beautiful creature that is intuitively tapped in and tuned into the harmonic resonance, the source of all creation, and how in the grand scheme of things it is bizarre and quite ridiculous that you would find yourself here, wavering between the desire to live and the desire to die...

You can see the "character" that you were playing, just like the role of an actress who was motivated by circumstances, crashing through life to find you'd landed yourself in quite the pickle...

*How does the character get out of this place? Where does the script lead you from here?*

You know this game. But unlike a script that is written and where the outcome is certain, in this story—your story—you get to choose the outcome. You get to decide how the story unfolds....

You have chosen life. With your arrival on this page, you have activated the will to survive, the will to live, the will to surrender to whatever it takes to pull yourself through the situation in which you find yourself. So good job! This is something that no one else can do for you. That willpower has to come from within you...and you claimed it!

The life force is now flowing to you, such that you are soon to find yourself full to overflowing with positivity, and soon you will see that *you* generate this flow of life force and that it is natural and easy and effortless...

You do not drain the unlimited supply, the divine source—it is infinite and it is all of creation. This healing energy is saturated with love and enriched with the codes of awakening. Love is energy. Love is light. Love is awareness.

As your body receives this infusion, there is a transformation happening deep in your cells, all the trillions of cells in your body. They are receiving this light as nourishment. They are vibrating in a subtle way that stirs them to align with the life force.

This infusion of the life force circulates into your consciousness, which in turn affects your thoughts and in turns affects your feelings. There is a calibration happening in your physical body—to have your body, mind and spirit resonate with existence. This is its natural state. Any living creature is designed to survive and exist…this is the base program. This is the modus operandi of a living organism. So for that to be shut off or disengaged means there is a dysfunction, an interference or a disruption in the mechanism of the survival instinct.

In this instance, there is the extraction of an entity…a gaseous, noxious form of darkness that had entered in through the back of your neck. It is being released into the light right now. This is a form of exorcism, a type of extraction of dark forces. This is one and there may be more, but this is a good first step. You may find your clarity of thought returns with this spirit banished.

As you clear "house," you allow more love, grace and light into your body…

Good job, my friend. With practice, you can become aware that these are things to be conscious of and how to banish them from your space.

This much, then, is enough for now.

*Yes!*

# Recreating Yourself

**D**EAR ONE,

As the energy opens in the session, I am compelled to take a long, slow deep breath… *ahhhhhhhhhhhhh.*

The guides that are here today would like to take a moment to acknowledge how far you have come by giving you a "pat on the back" of sorts. It is so clear how strong your voice is, how much you have cleared, and how anchored you are in yourself compared with the way you lived years ago.

Your voice is central to our work today. Whether it is in your astrological make-up or a skill that you came into the world with, your voice is a tool and a channel for the Divine power to come through you.

When you are feeling off balance, scattered or fragmented (you show me the particles of yourself fragmenting like a mirror breaking), find your voice. Feel whatever sounds want to come through you—with the intention that you are pulling the pieces of yourself back together.

It is important to note that once you have been obliterated into a billion fragments and have discovered the way to pull back the pieces of yourself into wholeness, that is when life brings you to the point of obliteration once again. But your soul knows what to do to regroup and restore. This pattern of blasting out into the universe across space and time is something that we do occasionally to cast the net wide, so to speak—to go "super nova," if you like—and scatter our particles across the heavens. Why? Because we can. And each time we do, we bring back information, transmissions, and the magic elixir of the hero's journey...to impart and share with others.

So rather than beat yourself up or flagellate yourself (you are not a Benedictine monk in this lifetime!) for falling down the rabbit hole and for being out of whack, celebrate that you are going through one of your cycles of obliteration!

And like the phoenix, a most magical being, you recreate yourself from the ashes once again...

When you have been reduced to ash and there is no form or no aspect of your "self" that remains, then the witness consciousness (the pure essence of you, the all-knowing, all-seeing, divine presence that resides deep within every human being) is able to recreate anew.

- How do you wish to recreate yourself?
- What qualities of the old self no longer serve your new form?
- What things can you leave behind in the ashes?
- What qualities do you wish to embrace?

Summon them, call them in! Is it courage? Is it clarity? Is it direction? Is it guidance? Is it stamina? Is it self-love?

Another way to think of this time is that your "blueprint holo-gram" temporarily goes offline while the glitches in the program are being rewritten. The kinks in the system are being ironed out. You are literally recreating yourself. It is natural to be in retreat when this process is happening, as you are literally morphing yourself.

And every time a life event or situation comes to you that expands you or pulls at your attention, you have the opportunity to see if it "fits" the new paradigm of your being. If it no longer resonates or "fits," then let it go. There may be some attachment to the energy that feeds into you from being "who you were" but this energy is minuscule to the energy that you have access to from within your own being to fill your own cup to overflowing.

I see the hoards like ravenous and caged pack animals, hungry for meat. You have lived enough lives where you were thrown to the wolves and torn asunder. Again, there's that pattern of obliteration that has been woven through your lifetimes and woven through your karma. In this life you are learning that you do not have to physically be obliterated to access the stars, to access the cosmic divine codes of healing....

Your consciousness is enough—your awareness is enough—your mindfulness that you are cycling through this process is enough to allow it to happen, to surrender to the fact that now you are reduced to ashes. This is when to rest and withdraw. You will know when to act, when to restore, when to present your being to the public as the full-feathered, glorious golden magical creature that has mouths open wide in wonder. The phoenix appears again, representing resurrection, renewal, *consecration* (being in service to the sacred).

You are alive for a reason!

Honor the time when you collapse into pieces. Honor the time when you are reduced to ashes. Honor the time when you rise and are being born anew. Honor the time when you are in your full glory.

*Yes!*

## 5 - 5

# RESTORATION

D EAR ONE,

As I write, a butterfly flutters up to the window and does a little dance. Butterfly medicine is here . . .

This is the medicine of transformation and recognizing where you are in that process. Are you the grub? Are you in a cocoon. Are you about to fly?

Remember, there is always more: more to explore, more depths to dive into, more expansion, more aspects of yourself to study and become aware of . . . and Spirit is asking of you that you once again expand the parameters of your bandwidth to hold a greater volume of power.

This growth is sometimes uncomfortable. Imagine what it must be like to be a pupa turning into a gloopy goo, completely regrowing your form. Nobody ever asked a butterfly if that is uncomfortable!

But remember: while this transformation is taking place, you are contained in a beautiful cocoon of love. This is what you are becoming aware of: the love you feel and know is only greater and greater and greater in its ability to express itself, and this is coming through you in new and beautiful ways.

And yes, there is the sadness in you that yearns to share that with someone you love who has transitioned—but take note, dear heart, they are dancing with you all the way, closer to you now than your very breath. They are consciousness itself, beyond form, pure creation, pure source, pure limitless love and there are no bounds here . . no end to the ways that it can be expressed to you, through you.

Every time you feel connected to the Source and that God power in you, you have access to all experience and all realities across space and time in the infinite now.

You ask for visiting hours to heaven and I say your wish is granted. They are there with you, in you, around you...of you. If you want to see them, ask them to come to you in a dream. It is possible to feel full from that dream as if it were real—*wink, wink*—really there is no difference. You have to remember that this reality is an illusion and that truly there is no here and there, or up and down and inside or out. Part of our evolution as a species is coming to know that in our bones . . . when you palpably experience it first hand, there can be no denying it.

"Ask and ye shall receive" . . . but don't wait by the phone. The timing of it is in the hands of the greater power, and it will come when you least expect it.

In the words of your direct guidance, "Be open to it..." Just as you have been so open to everything else, you will find that it flows effortlessly for you.

Now, envision a plumb line from the top of your head, correcting your vertical alignment and lifting you up from the sternum. Breathe deeply into your chest and lungs and allow yourself to be pulled upright from this part of your chest. *Tadasana* is the classic yoga standing pose where you practice this sense of lift.

And tune into the beautiful play of light around your throat chakra: there is some speaking or song or tone that wants to come through you. When you are feeling out of whack, try soothing yourself with your own voice, you may be surprised at what comes out and the effect of the vibration on your whole system. There is an adjustment happening to the volume of frequency that is coming to you and through you, shifting everything and moving you into the phase of transformation.

And it is as if your head is feeling somewhat disconnected from the rest of you, trying to wrestle with the information that is coming through. The trick is that you are not going to figure it out in your head—this is an all-body experience, so don't look for the answers in your mind.

You are right on track! You scheduled this ahead of time!

Follow this reading through with some form of bodywork, which is always helpful to ease the ride when you are in the thick of it and your physical form is adjusting to your expansion.

You will feel like you have come back to yourself in the next day or two, and returning to this reading, if you are so inclined, will assist with the integration of that vibration. Thank you for being so brave and courageous, and for being such a bright light.

*Yes!*

## 5 - 6

# YOU ARE PERFECT

Dear one,

In the grand scheme of things, there is no judgment. There is no approval or disapproval. There just is *what is*. And part of our evolution as a species is *acceptance*, acceptance that we are the way we are with all of our little idiosyncrasies and quirks. Whether we are fastidious or sloppy, fixated or spaced out, it is only the human mind that lays judgment on one way of being over another.

What if you were completely utterly perfect just as you are? And what if the universe and whole infinite spectrum of creation was in celebration of your existence, proud of your accomplishments, applauding your courage, ecstatic at your ability to look and see into the depths…

What if you were Creator itself looking through your eyes back at yourself? Realizing that *here you are* in the form of individuated consciousness, or your human costume, playing the game of life . . . how hysterical is that?

It feels pretty good actually . . . and then ego comes into play and says, "Wow, I'm really important and powerful, so look at me 'cause I'm awesome" and this is a trap of sorts...

Because once the ego or the "I" becomes involved with this super ecstatic awareness of itself as the Divine Source, and the power that comes with all of that, the polar opposite will flash across the screen of your mind, swinging to the other extreme when you least expect it. Because these negative thoughts are hardwired into the currents of your emotional body, when they sneak up on you, the physical body will react with a stress response: it will strain and contract and seek to restore balance, and it may feel temporarily depleted in the process.

So it is important to be aware that with every expansion of awareness, there is the following contraction. To be mindful that yes, you are human. Yes, you are tuning into your essence, and humility is a good thing. Some of the wisest, most enlightening souls are so very humble.

Free of the need to show some outer display, you can go super nova on the inside, and it is the best fireworks display ever. That is the best party, when your inner realm is so sparkly, blissful and joyful that it spills out of you in all that you do. No need to blow your own trumpet. It is obvious and apparent to all those around you who have the eyes to see and the ears to listen.

With the acceptance for who you are and gratitude for what you have and exactly where you are, all else can flow. The gifts from the universe know no bounds. In any moment, there is infinite possibility...

Yes, of course you have an idea of what you would like to manifest and create. This is your vision. Yet there is a subtle difference and a tangible flow of energy around wanting something you don't have versus being grateful for what you do have and allowing all things to flow.

Living in this realization, you find yourself experiencing ecstatic moments of joy at the simplest of things: a butterfly on a flower, a cool breeze, the taste of water, rays of sunlight, a child playing, and the list goes on. This state of being, this presence of mind, this experience of gratitude and delight is the holy grail, the jackpot, the lottery. All else flows from this place. This is your heart-generating love, manifesting love all around you.

This is why we have come here: to remember, to experience, and to assist others to remember....

So enjoy, in joy . . . yes.

Right now there is a clearing around your throat chakra, an unraveling of energy corkscrewed in at your throat. You may notice yourself clearing your voice in the next few days, and let yourself sing. Sound would like to come through you and it is healing and uplifting, as the vibration of sounds through your form fulfill you.

Sing . . . even if it is just to yourself.

*Yes!*

# Golden Release

D EAR ONE,

The spirit guides come bearing gifts of flowers and petals made of light in acknowledgement and as a thank-you for the work that you have been doing, knowing full well that you affect people's lives in a profound and magical way and that sometimes you may wonder if it is enough. Well, the unseen realms are here to say, "Yes and Thank You!" And by seeing this flow of gratitude coming to you from the spirit realm, it is an activation of the reciprocity that comes from doing this work, allowing you to receive the gifts that you have worked hard to earn…

They are unraveling the energy around your throat chakra. I see you clearing your throat—as if your experience through the past few months has created a contraction in your throat and a need to speak your truth, but feeling like there was no opening or "listening" to hear what you had to say from the person who is on your mind right now.

This energy then brings attention to the feeling you have

experienced of actually having hands around your throat at one point, either in this lifetime or another, even to the point of extinguishing your life force in another dimension. And so there is a total squirminess in your body that is wriggling under that force (naturally as one would be if one was experiencing that) and that squirminess is seeking release also. That energy has kind of appeared like an overlay (as if someone had drawn a picture on some trace paper and placed it over your body) and there is a feeling of your body and spirit being trapped under this layer...

Your relationship to this person is karmic. The dynamic that is being played out is a "residue" of a much more intense situation from another time. Only this time you have a whole different bag of tools and are in a very different place to be able to deal and grow from the learning. We are removing that layer and thanking this person for creating the situation in which you could now examine that. Everything is absolutely appropriate as you know and even though it has been difficult, their presence acts as a catalyst for everyone to take their healing and their evolution to the next level. So shedding the layers of the old karmic binds allows you to be on the "surgeon's table," so to speak—to shine the light into your consciousness and see where you are at in order to express your best self...

And it is a beautiful self indeed! I truly hope that you can see how beautiful you are. There is a childlike joy and playfulness in your being that radiates like a jewel. I'm sure that others who come to see you and work with you and learn from you have this awakened in themselves.

So yes, we're removing this layer—it's kind of like peeling off sticky plastic wrap from all around you. It has definitely been dampening the life force and suffocating your energy field. The guides are disappearing that in a puff of smoke—*kapow!*

There is a release that comes with this, and tears may need to come. Please just allow them, remembering that it takes about three days to integrate and you may be feeling upside down for a few days.

But you are free! Free of the binds, free of the suffocation and the smothering. Take deep breaths in the next few days—breathe in the fresh air outside.

With this clearing comes a *Zing!* that travels from your solar plexus up through your heart and into your voice. Do you sing? Tone? Speak? There is a deep golden glow in your belly, a super-powered ball of goodness that wants to travel up through your body and out. You show me your arms outstretched, surrounded by gold sparkly stars and the angels by your side dancing and whirling swirling and generating a beautiful current that nurtures the people who come to you.

And now I see the vortex energy at the back of your neck, the counter balance to the throat. It has also been pulled in and contracted. Spirit shows me the analogy of pulling on a thread for a piece of fabric—when you pull on one thread, the whole piece of fabric gets pulled or distorted. We are restoring balance now to the energy at the back of your neck—it is kind of like a wheel alignment, but for the front and back of your neck. It would be great if you could get someone to press into the top of your trapezius muscles. I feel those muscles all bunched up. Either receive a massage or lie on a tennis ball. The chiropractor is a perfect person to visit after this reading, as an adjustment anchors the energy into your cells…and helps with the integration.

From this alignment comes a beautiful glow from your heart—like your heart energy generator has been reactivated and engaged. It also had been dampened.

With this comes a clarity of thought too—and gold is your color today! You are showing me golden glow in your brain and head and mind, which shoots out of your third eye in white light and sparks.

So much of this is about flipping the reciprocity switch in your being, so that you can physically embody the gifts that are coming to you from spirit and hold the vibration of receiving that beautiful golden energy. You have earned it and Spirit would like very much for you to receive your rewards in the physical. You show me a giggle and a secret smile to yourself, because you know how hard you have worked and are working and you really do know how to manifest (you are a master at manifestation). You show me it raining gold and coins on you in a shower of prosperity! You are dancing and skipping joyfully, and much of this prosperity is intricately tied to your joy. It is like you manifest from that place, and when your "joy-o-meter" is dampened it reflects in the real world....

So here's food for thought: when there is a lull or a slowing of people coming to soak in that golden energy, find the thread of joy in you. Do something for you that brings you joy and makes you happy, and it will reboot and reactivate the infinity symbol of reciprocity in your being.

Please be kind to yourself in the next few days. Treat yourself as if you have just had surgery—be *gentle, gentle, gentle* and enjoy things that are nurturing to your body, like herbal tea and flowers and hot baths. Call in the divine Mother Mary, as she is here now in the session to walk with you; and Michael also has his sword drawn in the golden light to hack away any threads that come your way. It is good that your attention has been drawn to the layer that was upon you because now you can see it, know it was there and be aware if it starts to feel like that again—because you can disappear it yourself. That is not to say it will happen again, you just want to remain aware.

Connect to the beautiful golden energy that you generate. Bring that down into your legs, through the knees and into the Earth so your whole body is surrounded in gold and flowing with gold...

Thank you for your beautiful work.

*Yes!*

# SIXTH CHAKRA
*Trust Your Vision*

**6 - 1**

# The Liberation of Surrender

**D**EAR ONE,

The word that comes through straight away is "Clarity."

With this is a honing of your third eye and an opening at the base of your skull (the atlas or occipital ridge) so that the energy can flow from your heart through this area of vital life force up into your brain.

Across the mechanism that is your nervous system—all of the pathways and branches and the currents that flow through it—information is being sent back and forth to the brain all the time. It is truly remarkable, this critical flow that goes largely unnoticed unless there is pain.

Right now, bring your attention to the vital energy that is coursing through your neck. The spinal cord and your major arteries feed up into your brain. The cerebral cortex, the grey matter or higher functioning part of your brain, is the focus now. Many suggest that this is in fact the house of "awareness." It is essential to have the energy flow to this part of you for maximum clarity.

Many of us walk around with our heads jammed so tightly onto our necks that it staunches that flow. As you fall asleep each night, allow your head to feel as heavy as a bowling ball and sink deep into the pillow. By doing so, you are focusing your awareness on the tension in your spinal cord and allowing your entire body to relax.

While any mental catharsis that you have been experiencing is perfect, it is time to remember that every time you lie down to sleep, you carry the entire day's stresses with you. It is neither necessary nor productive to bring them into the dream state. It is good to consciously let them go so that your body can completely regenerate and restore.

So with these words we celebrate and tune into your nervous system, sweeping this field to clear any blockages and tangles associated with glitches or misfiring information, affecting your clarity of thought. This unraveling at the base of your skull will feel like a great pressure has been lifted off your shoulders, a weight that has been bearing down on you.

Connected to this is a need to speak your truth that has somehow been choked off—you know the meaning of this in your heart.

Always with this work is a gradual surrendering to the truth. Is there a part of you that has been fooling yourself, telling yourself one thing, when deep down you know in your heart that it is not so? What is this revelation? It yearns to come forth and now it is ready for you to see—it is time.

Are you afraid of acknowledging this truth? Perhaps it is as simple as realizing that you are magnificent and you have been fooling yourself to believe otherwise. You have been fed a lie by yourself, and a part of you is sad to acknowledge this. Any resistance, frustration or discontent is the last-ditch effort to hang onto this falsity with which you have identified for a long time. Even though it is crusty and gritty, there is comfort in its familiarity and a complacency in settling for a menial existence.

It is time to raise the bar, my friend. It is time—and your spirit has designated this time in space—to seize the reins and make the conscious choice to be the best that you can be. The joke is that you have already activated the switch so there's no turning back. And now the residue ick is the last bastion of your ego fighting to remain "in control"...ha...

You may have seen the beautiful expression being passed around the web:

"Relax, nothing is under your control."

And come to a crossroads where we think "*F#)$ this S*#&$", I'm the boss here, it's my life and I'm holding the reins. All kinds of data surface in our minds about control and conformity and we fight and we fight and we fight and ultimately we are only fighting ourselves....

And of course the cosmic joke is that as soon as we surrender to the greater power and hand it all over to the Creator—we surrender to our truth, we align with our purpose and doors open everywhere—the result is inexplicable joy.

If your system has been programmed with Catholic church data about a judgmental Creator who will condemn you if you sin and send you to hell if you don't conform, I'd like to suggest that there is a bigger picture—and that it is OK to step outside of that mental construct, that narrow bandwidth of perception or belief.

Perhaps just perhaps, Creator is all of it: the dark, the light, the yin the yang, the beauty, the pain, and there is no judgment, there is no right or wrong—*it just is what it is* and the love of Creator is woven through all of it. You, me, everything that exists.... All of it...

So breathe, relax your spinal cord and know that *deep* transformation is at hand, such deep transformation that your very form is changing shape from the inside out. This can be unsettling. Sensitivities are amplified. It is OK to want to retreat into your cocoon or home space. It is OK if the work load wanes a little. The universe does work in mysterious ways: when the work load lessens, it is time to give back to yourself. Do the things you love that nurture your spirit, allow yourself the time and space to enjoy doing them, and feel the expanse of this allowance. This is sinking deeper into that trust...

This is the Trust that comes with the surrender...you will find a way through.

Give yourself a pat on the back for how far you have come...it is not easy to look into the depths, it is not easy to clear out the psychic debris. You are working on this 24/7!

With this reading, you have put yourself in the washing machine and you have been in a spin cycle! This too shall pass, and you will come out squeaky clean.

Layer upon layer, as much as you can handle in any given moment, it is all appropriate. You are right on track. You are doing great. And if you need a good wail at the moon occasionally, go for it. Nothing like a good heart-aching sob with the release of tears to cleanse the soul. It is appropriate to grieve for the end of this chapter of your life, the end of this identification with the ego.

Recognize that you are the dream and the Dreamer. Recognize that you are the One you've been looking for. Recognize that you are Creator in human form (blasphemy!) experiencing life in the humblest way as your divine self, that you are worthy of your own love, and that you are worthy of receiving. And the greatest treasure, the greatest gift, the holy grail is that of surrendering to the truth of Who You Are...

It's celebration time.

Life is precious, life is golden, life is sacred—life is a gift. You have been chosen and you have chosen to awaken.

Now is the time...

*Yes!*

# REGENERATION

D EAR ONE,

You are inviting a fine tuning, a recalibration of your energy field, a process that is especially enhanced as you sit in mediation, eyes closed, breathing into yourself.

You can tune into the very oscillation of your own existence: night and day, up and down, left and right, inhale and exhale.

Your heartbeat ripples out in a wave which is also a coherent oscillation or wave form each time you allow the mind to be quiet and focus on that resonance within you. With this, you are allowing that oscillation to increase its amplitude and regularity versus being at the mercy of external forces that can knock you off center and interfere with your calm.

This awareness is about you generating your own power and vibration that affects everyone in your field, rather than you being at the mercy of everyone else.

During this fine tuning of your focus to bring your attention to this resonance, your mind will want to slip into its habitual *"blah, blah, blah"* as you sit at first; but the more you practice it, the easier it will become to still that chatter and zero into the frequency of your own being.

Before you engage with folks or relatives or anyone who is an energetic drain, bathe yourself in the Violet Flame, an ancient archetypal tool to protect and shield yourself from anyone "hooking in" to you. Just visualize yourself bathed in violet flames until you are immersed in and at one with them. Violet is the highest vibration, the end of the spectrum of visible color to the human eye and it in effect aligns you with the most life-affirming frequency by doing this.

And in this place of stillness and silence, the mind becomes still and you punch through the "veil" and your spirit is free…free to journey and gather knowledge and wisdom, because here you are tapped into the Big Picture and can see beyond the restrictions of space and time. It is also possible to reunite with loved ones in this place to continue the dance with them there.

Happening now is an unraveling of energy at the back of your neck (on the occipital ridge). It's as if you have been "under the thumb," pushing your head and chin forward and probably creating strain on your trapezius muscles and shoulders. Imagine a corkscrew of energy: when turned one way, it creates a contraction, when rotated in the other direction, it creates an expansion. You can keep *visually* unscrewing this if or when you are feeling like your neck is stiff or you have a headache. As for which way to turn the energetic screw, you will know which way to unscrew the energy as the effect will be instantaneous relief. The direction is different for each body—just as a pendulum swings clockwise as *Yes* for one person, it may also swing counterclockwise as *Yes* for another. You will know which way feels like it is unraveling. And it is a good practice to tune into that flow of energy as it will help you understand how your energy wants to move.

Also, take some deep breaths into this area—it shifts the energy immensely, releasing "the weight" of recent weeks you have been carrying. Give your body some appreciation and acknowledgement for functioning at full capacity and doing everything you needed it to do under extreme duress. Recognize that it has been serving you well! In addition, do some things that bodies love: sleep in, take a hot bath, get a massage, receive acupuncture, stretch or dance. Yes, it's time to honor the body that has carried you through this entire chapter.

Finally, turn conscious attention to your third eye, the chakra (energy vortex) in the center of your brow, which is opening. When you sit in meditation, it is a good time to allow your eyes to roll towards your brow and focus your attention there. This is your inner vision, and this opening allows you to read energy with your "mind's eye." So if you start to notice subtle changes in your perception, you are not mistaken. Trust those flashes and observations because they are the beginnings of awakening to the world beyond the visible world.

Notice. The next time you are in a dimly lit room, you may begin to discern the energy field around a form, whether human or animal, and as you get better at it, even around inanimate objects. This is the energy imprint of a particular form. You can see it even around your own hands, and of course all around you. With the third eye open, you can start to sense and "see" the energy and life force of a being. So in this way, it opens you to experiencing reality in a different way. It's like having another tool in your awareness kit.

Lastly take a moment (or many moments) to acknowledge the role of friends who have supported you, as you, as of late. Sing to them. It will comfort you and it will be an expression of your deepest most sacred offering. No matter the words or the tune, just allow whatever wants to come through in the moment, as you close your eyes...

Recharge. Refuel. Recalibrate.

*Yes!*

# CLARITY OF MIND

D EAR ONE,

The first words that come when I tune into you are: *clarity of mind.* And then you show me the Archetype of Atlas, carrying the world upon your shoulders.

This reflection is about shrugging off that weight and standing tall—back to being on top of the world. You are empathic and sensitive to others in turmoil and have absorbed some energies from people around you in chaos. It starts as a tweak in your neck, spreads across your traps, and pretty soon you've just gotten used to that constant nagging discomfort or numbed to that tension—and your whole back is rigid and locked and you can't remember when it started.

A massage will help integrate, into your cells, what is now transpiring for you.

Recently you've been asked to step outside your comfort zone, to make some tough decisions, or to be firm in dealing with people, whether family or coworkers. This has created an inner turmoil in you, as it doesn't resonate with your familiar groove. Know that you are "character building" right now and in retrospect will see that this period of time is an important cycle of growth and expansion into the fullness of Who You Are.

With this bring focus upon your neck, the part "holding up the whole world." There is unraveling and a corkscrew action in the top three vertebrae, including the atlas. Breathe "YES" into this area each time you remember in the next three days—the release here will bring you a flood of clarity, with decision processes restored to sharp and quick.

Spirit is linking this energy line into your heart with much grounding, in through your feet, bringing up energy so that it is circulating throughout your whole system. If you've been feeling spacey, it because it's as if you'd skipped out through the top of your head. It is good to ground or practice "earthing" for half an hour a day: just walk barefoot on the Earth and allow your energy to flow into the ground and then open to receive it coming back.

Even as all this is good, clarity of mind remains the predominant theme. It is time to reboot. No surprise if you dozed off. Deep exhaustion is apparent. It's time to drop all the rah rah and go for a bike ride or take a mental health day. Sit in a spa, climb to a mountain top, or just shake up the routine and break the cycle of the "holding it all together" treadmill.

You show me literally shaking water from your head, resurfacing— and there is cosmic humor in that word. You are resurfacing from being "underwater" with the load of recent times...so go swim! If there is no beach, then go to the pool! There is a caution here, from Spirit, knowing your tendency to get swept up in work and brush rest off as not important. You have given yourself this time to read, yet this is the tip of the iceberg for the real work begins as you integrate the Spirit Guidance here.

Your left eye lights up. Spirit is working here on both eyes, but mainly your left one for clarity of vision—if not physically, then metaphysically. Now is a good time to take stock and reassess your vision for your next chapter, not only for yourself but as a family, and then the bigger global family comes in too. Yes, I see you hold a grand vision for the planet! Please dream that dream and practice envisioning that, as you are literally creating that as a possible future for all of us and adding to the golden web that the rest of us light workers tap into. Please do not underestimate the power of your ability to manifest.

Ah, you show me *you* taking a huge deep breath and sigh of relief. Yes, it feels good to get the planet off your back! You are of greater service to all of humanity when you are not carrying it and absorbing it in your physical body.

Don't be surprised if the world looks different after today. And don't worry, you only "get" as much as you can handle. The growth is incremental and exponential. This last period has been an enormous push through the fabric of your old reality, kind of like being born anew…

Please treat yourself as new. Be kind to yourself. Shake it up and go play, take a day off, wail at the moon if you need to, enjoy a beer with friends, cut yourself some slack, make love, get on a merry-go-round…

The archangels also here with you and you'll be feeling on top of the world in no time.

*Yes!*

# HIGHER VISION

D EAR ONE,

Today you are showing me that your right eye is the eye that sees and feels the pain around you and that your left eye is the one that anchors you to your spirit. It is strong and true and focused and deep in that eye I see your spirit blazing bright.

And in the right eye, it is as if you have been burned so badly that there is that 'cringing' sensation of retreating from intense amount of pain. So this divide creates a sort of schism in your being. Where on one hand you are ready to take on the world and you feel overwhelming love awe at all the beauty around you, on the other you are deeply affected by the pain that you see, everywhere, in everything and everyone.

So it is as if you are seeking safe haven.

I would recommend to you that you find yourself a path to visit a sanctuary for the spirit, an ashram, a shrine to the temple of the heart. It feels like you just need some respite from the world in a place that will hold your spirit in a sacred space where all baggage is left at the door.

I also see the spiral unlocking of the throat chakra and a stream of toxicity and vile language that is kind of stuck there. Today we are clearing a serpent entity that is wrapped around your throat. Perhaps you have been witness to that toxicity or the recipient of that or the deliverer, or all three…yet I see spitting and hissing and intense venom being spat out through words, and it is jabbing and striking and angry.

This energy is in an infinity symbol that creates a feedback loop, so whether you have been the one projecting this or receiving this, either way or both, it lands in your soft tissue. Apart from the vertebrae in your neck, most of the neck region is soft tissue and all of the vital organs pass through this passage…it is what connects your head to your body, yes, but it is also what allows your consciousness to ground into reality.

So this serpent wrapped around your neck is a good thing to see and reveal, as it has been acting as a kind of filter to your experience of reality.

Did anyone ever put their hands around your throat? Was there violence? If not in this life, then another where that was perhaps your end. It is like you have come into this body having transferred that experience over as a distant echo. And by coming in with that in your energy field it is then amplified and rebounding all through your field.

With that constriction in the throat it is then pinging around in your head as "broken beyond repair," allowing the thought patterns to loop and affect your waking life. I can see how it has been difficult to get a handle on those thoughts and stay connected to the loving feelings that you feel.

So with the lifting of this entity, there is a flooding of warmth throughout your entire body and a tingling sensation that may come as a result of nerve endings being engaged and fluid conductivity being restored. And now you show me your heart bursting onto the scene. And what a huge heart you have—so very large in its energy field. You show me that the lower right quadrant (or left if looking from the outside) is in shadow. So I ask you to send this part of your heart some love and light in the most creative way you can.

In fact, paint that. Paint your consciousness sending the lower left quadrant of your heart love and light. It will actively fortify this energy that is coming through now…

And do whatever you need to do to treat this as an assignment, rather than blow it off. Because instead of earning a grade or a credit, you will be earning merit and taking action to reclaim your power. And this is no joke. I'm sure that you can come up with a million reasons why not to do this. I am sure you can come up with a dozen distractions and stories as to why it's not important or relevant or that it doesn't matter. Watch the squirmy distaste that you feel for taking this project on, because it is everything inside of you that is resisting the call for you to shine in your light.

Start with a sketch. Watch the thoughts that surface as you draw. Face the empty canvas with this mission statement: notice the fear and repulsion and angst and all the negative thoughts and feelings that surface when you are given this task.

But know this: This assignment is given to you directly from your Higher Self. From your own radiant spirit. This is what your spirit is asking for you to do to break free, to start the wheels in motion and to lift you from the mire. This action will bring in more light, more love, more healing…more power. And through the project you will come to know your heart. You will come to heal the shadow that resides there. And you have asked for this by showing up to this reading.

Please affirm and make a promise to yourself that you will take this on.

Know that you have a legion of light behind your decision to take this action. Your commitment to your own healing is endorsed by the unseen realms, with a full stamp of approval from Creator. Ha, ha—the divine really does have a sense of humor when it comes to how seriously we take ourselves!

*Yes!*

# A HEALING FROM THE EARTH

D EAR ONE,
*Pachamama, Earth Mama, Gaia....*
She comes through straight away, very, very strong. Ooooh, today you are receiving a healing from the Earth herself.

Yes, it is a wave that flows through your entire being and harmonizes with that tremble in you. It undulates your whole body until the wave is both stronger and deeper, so in a sense you are carried by the wave—rather than shaking, trembling bobbing on the surface, you become one with that wave...and you are riding it, too.

Thumbs up, victorious. Your spirit is showing me that you are victorious!

Clarity...ask for clarity. Clarity on direction. Clarity on support. Clarity on security. Clarity on the finances, so that you know where you stand. I see that the "not knowing" about the finances is like a thick, foggy cloud in your consciousness and it floats around your head and with it breeds the voice of uncertainty and doubt.

Then this "voice" entwines in your entire body and nervous system like an octopus and pulls and jumps and starts so that your body jumps and skips like a puppet on a string.

So hold the vision of you riding the most beautiful crystal clear wave with your thumbs up in celebration, standing strong in the most exhilarating ride....as the wave takes you safely to shore.

We are clearing the cloud. The dove is clearing the cloud. The dove is a real and palpable symbol to show you there can be no doubt of the magic that is possible for you to experience and create. At first we often question, "Did that just happen?" or "did I make that up?" We are afraid to assign meaning to the messages from Spirit....because we are not taught to listen from an early age. As children we are taught to doubt our instincts. We are taught to doubt ourselves and our power and our connection to the all and everything. And every trauma or abuse or negative influence in the pool that we grew up in only strengthens and solidifies this doubt.

In the vision of you on that wave, you are ecstatically happy and blissfully alive and free. And you keep on showing me that vision.

So as a young woman you gravitate towards what you know and what is familiar to you as a "modal" or default in relationship. You are literally magnetized to a vibration that matches your own. Then something happens to you and you experience some form of awakening and you are shown a glimpse of something far sweeter and richer and more fulfilling and it is natural that you would yearn for that sweetness and that connection—the old vibration is no longer fulfilling you at the level of your essence. Really it is your soul that is yearning to be free and fully expressed and liberated...but the little girl in you is afraid. So it is a good time to recognize and nurture the little girl in you. She is afraid of the unknown.

This is the deep threads of emotion in you, also water…also pulsing through you in a wave form. So there is a reminder from a session before to be open to understanding and knowing yourself with your whole body, not just your mind. Let your body be your guide, and your spirit through your body—that way, you will choose the path that is in alignment with your highest purpose.

So when you are feeling shaky or off balance, find a quiet moment and sit with your hands on your belly and breath into the shakiness. Lie down if you need to, and let the shaking pulse through you. You can exaggerate it if you need…think of it as a vibrational attunement. Focus your mind on your breath and breathe into the source of the shaking. This is a way of allowing you to shed the light and examine an area of your consciousness. It may be uncomfortable, but just notice what feelings are there…just allow them to be. Allow them to surface. These feelings are what are keeping you in a place of stasis and uncertainty while they remain buried.

You are such a tremendously strong person, this much is clear. And you have the strength of the entire planet behind you.

Earth Mama. She is with you. You can draw on her strength when you are feeling vulnerable or unsure, just draw the energy up through your feet from the Earth and allow it to pour out of your heart. So when the fears arise of "Can I do this?"—remember that strength available to you in an instant.

And the message is no matter what that you will find your way.

So a prayer here then, for ease and effortlessness on your path, so that you are held and carried gently while given the lessons that you need to expand yourself. Remember that obstacles and challenges are opportunities for us to grow and learn the lessons that we need to be more fully whole. (Easy to say in retrospect but annoying when you are in the thick of it!) Spirit will give you little signs and symbols along the way to keep you enchanted and to follow the path of light, the path of the heart, the path of triumph.

So yes, now you are receiving a beautiful, warm, golden heart infusion of goodness from the angels and Michael steps forward with his sword to cut the cords that were having you be controlled. If you feel a little crumpled and disheveled in the next few days, fear not! You don't need the strings anymore and you are learning to flex the muscles so that you can stand and move on your own two feet. It is ok to be floppy for a few days while you adjust! This is an important part in your liberation from doubt. Sleep if you need to. Drink lots of water. Quench your thirst for clarity...I suspect as you begin to unravel information, you will find a curiosity in you that drives deep and wants to get to the bottom of it, like a mystery novel.

Know where you stand so that you can make a decision with all of the facts, so that you are playing with the whole deck of cards.

Lastly, Earth, Gaia, Pachamama is grounding you, grounding you deep into her soil and rocks and stone so that you feel anchored in yourself. Your foundations are strong and unwavering. You are powerful to call on her as your support—your inner shaman is emerging! Yes, it is so exciting to see you stretch and flex your wings. Trembling is also power coursing through you....

You are accessing your power. Ancient wisdom. Embedded in your cells.

Ride the wave...victorious.

*Yes!*

# Shining Light into the Depths

**D**EAR ONE,

Thank you for making the conscious decision to dive deep into the layers of your being, and for having the courage to look—to really, really look inside and see.

To shine the light into the depths is an act of *great* courage. For it requires a willingness to examine the places in us that would rather remain in shadow, the aspects of ourselves that would squirm and wriggle away, into the nooks and crannies to avoid exposure and hide out, to remain as a presence backstage and act as a mechanism of derision and divisiveness lurking in the darkness to blast onto center stage when we least expect it or subtly manipulate the workings of the stage from behind the curtain.

So in this way, you are taking the reins of your life. You are investigating what is the mechanism that creates that effect at the front on stage. You are walking into the creepy, dark corners with a blazing light behind you to shine the light and see, really see what is there....

So that you may witness it, recognize it and see it for what it is—and from this place you are able to affect the greatest change. You are able to acknowledge aspects of yourself that you might find distasteful or repulsive and let them go....

With awareness as your sharpest tool, you are equipped as a warrior of light—unafraid and willing to recognize, express and release that which no longer serves you.

Perhaps these mechanisms have existed to defend you, protect you, and shield you from harm—placed there during childhood?—only to surface and repeat a pattern of behavior that has served you until now....

And here at this point in your life—where you recognize that there is more you wish to have to fulfill you, more that you wish to know to satiate the thirst and the yearning—there is a wave of gratitude that I feel, a veritable tsunami of love that washes upon your shore... to lift your spirit and place you upon your throne of majesty, where you may claim your rightful place among the high priests and priestesses of the world. The memory of all of the lifetimes of service and devotion that are available to you, now, to access:

Earth power....

Divine conduit....

Holy Grail....

Holy Communion....

These words are, in fact, codes of activation that will ignite the spark of recognition and remembrance in you.

This remembering, this infusion of light—this surge of power is what you have been thirsty for, for some time...

You are accustomed to wielding great power in other dimensions through space and time—and really in all parallel universes, there is no such thing so it is here and now! Recognizing this gives you access...

And yet you find yourself in a body and a life that feels like your wings are clipped or your power is thwarted every which way you turn, like there is a wall or an obstacle. Remember the '80s computer snake game? It is as if you navigate the playing field as the snake gets longer and more difficult to maneuver until eventually you crash into your own tail...as life goes on and on, it becomes faster and faster and longer and longer...until BAM!

It is so good to see that and recognize the "playing field" or the mental construct that you find yourself in before you crash into your tail....

Because what is on offer here is to change it up, to step outside of the old construct and the old thought patterns and the old paradigm, to shake S@#T up.

And now you show me an Etch A Sketch—as if you are shaking up the picture you have drawn to clear the way for a new drawing....

These symbols, from an earlier time are representations. These references are never given without purpose. If there is a link to a memory, it is intentional. It is the drawing out of the slimy muck that is connected to these reference points as an emotional charge... it is your spirit guides being the snake charmer to the cobra or the pied piper luring out the rats...to allow the creepy crawlies to pour out of you....

Again, allow for three days for yourself to integrate after every reading. If you find that you are feeling toxic or vitriolic, take yourself for a walk on the beach, exercise and breathe it out of your system with the increase in heart rate—and be conscious that it does not lash out at the obvious targets (those closest to you).

But owning your own stuff—taking response-ability for your own lurking shadow—is a monumental step for the whole of existence. It takes the weight of blame and guilt and shame off "other," casting them in the light of compassion and kindness versus feeding and fueling the force of self-destruction.

So already, there is a tremendous shift in you. Already you are adept at working the energy. It is effortless for you because you are traversing time and space and accessing the lifetimes of accumulated knowledge, experience and wisdom. You got this!

You have claimed your right to sit amongst those that serve the highest good, just by showing up today…so good job!

Yar—and then there is the emotional wake that follows such an infusion – where you may feel like an obliterated blob of chaos. Enjoy that too! Juice it, revel in it for what it is, the clearing of muck, the relinquishment of control….

In that release is the deluge of hysterical, crazed and controlling anger that is no longer welcome in the house…

Your house. Your body. Your show. Your life. Your act. Your reality.

Filling the house with grace. Filling the house with peace. Filling the house with light…releasing the muck that lurks and feeds on the emotional charge that lays hidden…until now….

Be free!

And know that by owning your part, you bring light and grace and peace for everyone.

By releasing this flow of energy, you bring clarity to your thoughts, clarity to your heart, clarity to your purpose….

*Yes!*

# THE POWER TO DREAM
# WHO YOU ARE

D EAR ONE,

Allow yourself a moment to shine the light on a dream and a vision of yourself as healed and whole and magnificent and radiant and successful and fulfilled and in love and alive and blissful.

And then notice what wants to stifle that vision?

How long can you hold it?

Is it a fleeting nanosecond?

Can you even find it?

You are an artist. You can bring it through, I have faith in you. You have not lost the power to dream and imagine.

These tools are innate in your being—this is a skillset you were born with. You didn't have to learn them from any school or teacher; you came into this life with that kit.

Your homework is this:

Ask yourself:

Who am I?

Who do I dare to be?

Who do I dare to dream that I am?

And feel the tinge of excitement that follows those thoughts and that line of questions. Because that tinge of excitement is the thread that we will follow as we work together. That tinge of excitement is your lifeline. That tinge of excitement is your link to a life that is fulfilled and hopeful and lived in grace and in love and in the light.

Can you see that your thought patterns have you held in a loop of self-destruction and self-annihilation? And thus your waking hours are "cringing" and you feel barely able to make it through the next moment.

Call on your guardian angel, who shines through you so very, very brightly. Our job here is to allow you to see it and feel it and know it in your bones…because that is what you are. You are here to assist others who are stuck in the mire and the muck by reaching out a hand to help them up. Through your art. Through your presence. Through you sharing yourself.

Your beauty is not just surface. Your light is radiant. Part of your internal struggle and despair is that you have been disconnecting from yourself as a spirit. You have been unable to see yourself as this magnificent light. But it is plain as day to me. All else is just peripheral fluff that can fall away like an old skin. So fear not…there is more than great hope for you. You are not a lost cause (as I'm sure you have told yourself time and time again).

Be mindful of that internal monologue. We can be our own worst enemy. That is the ego talking that wants to keep you small and wants to keep you stuck and trapped and down.

This work that we have embarked upon today is the deepest and most profound kind of work a person can do. It is the work of the evolution of the soul. It is the work of recognizing yourself as a radiant spark of the divine and allowing *that* to fill your physical body to such an extent that you can no longer have any doubt or any reason to question yourself or your role here.

So, thank you. And I mean that from the deepest wellspring in my heart. Thank you for having the courage to look and see and face the depths of your being and all of the icky shit in there that has had you running in circles for so long. It really does take a tremendous amount of courage to turn and put the spotlight on your consciousness and see what is running you from the deepest depths. And it ain't all pretty and it ain't all light and fluff.

So even if from today you walk away by patting yourself on the back—opening this door and starting with the first step of taking a deep dive and examining who you are—that is a monumental step. Can you see that and recognize that you have just done that by showing up today? Easy huh? The work is really no harder than that. Showing up and being prepared to receive what you need to hear to grow and learn and spread those giant angel wings that are tucked neatly up out of sight. At present only those with the eyes to see can see them. But there is a way here to let them reveal for all to see.

There is no shame in asking for help. Some people will go through their whole lives without exploring all of their options. Some people will take their own lives because they believe there are no options. You are lucky. And you will come to know down the line that with this door that is opening comes a responsibility and a service to others.

What a concept, hey? That you would be helping others? "How can that be when I am such a mess?" you might ask yourself. And we are asking you to hold that thread of excitement, that tinge, that tingle in your body that you may well feel as a pulse or a shiver or a wave or a surge of emotion in the next few days because it is the feeling that we are exploring here that is your path to freedom...personally, creatively, globally....

I want to speak to the situation on the planet right now for people such as yourself who have come from so very far away where everything is light and energy and harmonious and in tune with a beautiful resonance:

It is easy to feel the weight of everything here that is wrong and messed up and desperately sad. And it is easy to stifle that feeling too, because sometimes it is too much to bear. Sometimes it is too much to contain in one body. Especially a body that houses a spirit that is used to functioning on a much higher light vibration.

And the words that you need to hear are: "You do not have to carry the weight of the world."

Own your power. Own your magnificence. Own your light. Own your love and share that through your work and your presence. In this way, you make the greatest impact on the entire world. This is your contribution. Everybody that witnesses your work and your being receives a transmission of light when you walk in balance and harmony in your own being. You become the catalyst for the healing of others and the catalyst for the evolution of their spirit.

Now this is all very lofty stuff and the "ego" wants to grab a hold of it and say, "Yeah, I'm amazing and so freakin' important" and yada yada yada....

But this is way beyond ego. This inner wisdom is really the most humbling experience you can have. And that humility shows in little ways and in everything you do....

The ego will destroy you as fast as it puts you on a pedestal. So this is not to put you on a pedestal so that your shadow side can tear you to shreds—this is to bring your awareness to your essence to the light within you that is so very, very bright.

Congratulations!

You have initiated your pathway to the light—it is like following the yellow brick road to find the wizard behind the curtain and you find that you actually already you have everything you need to bring you back home, back home to yourself.

Notice how you feel in the next few days. I encourage you to journal your thoughts, dreams, body sensations. My motto in life has always been "the lower the lower, the higher the high that follows"... and it has been very true. You can imagine what is possible given the time you have spent in hell. Yes, hell is here on Earth. We are creating heaven on Earth—together. It is a state of mind. It is a state of being. It is when we become the bridge between Heaven and Earth and hold the balance as a divine conduit, this is holy communion. This is bliss. This is a life fulfilled and ecstatic to be alive. This is a life lived in service and surrender to our divine being connected to Creator and basking in the love of God.

Can you imagine? Even for just a fleeting moment! Hold that thought! Hold that vision!

We are opening the aperture of your awareness to put this vision in center frame. And we are casting away the murky mire of muck that no longer serves you or your family or the planet...you can be done with that—hallelujah!

Today you have received an important activation. A vibration of healing energy.

Allow any catharsis that needs to come out come out.

Scream and yell into a pillow.

Let the tears come.

Wrap yourself in cotton wool.

Walk in the forest.

Sit by the ocean or a river.

Fill yourself up with negative ions given to us through nature.

Belt out that punk rock song that wants to rage at the indignity of life here on Earth.

PAINT!

And yes, of course, life will continue to throw you curve balls.

And you will continue to crack your way out of your cocoon.

The healing and liberation of your spirit is incremental as you receive as much as you can integrate in one session at a time. If all of the lights were to go on in your consciousness at the same time, it would fry your circuitry. So gently does it. Layer upon layer of opening to infinite possibility, infinite love and guidance. Starting today.

This much then is enough for now.

Your Cosmic Upgrade is complete. The song I've produced by this name[3] came on at the end of the session, another vibrational attunement.

---

3   "Cosmic Upgrade" is available at www.VisionWeaving.com.

Please consider listening to this in the next few days, to assist the integration of this energy.

Blessings to you, dear heart....

*Yes!*

# SEVENTH CHAKRA
*Awaken to Divine Nature*

## 7-1

# COSMIC UPGRADE

EAR ONE,

Attention is drawn to your crown chakra—it's as if in clearing out the old muck, literally and figuratively, and then putting into practice the soul lesson that has been processed in two recent events (which are interwoven and no accident that they happened in a short space of time), you have anchored in a new level of Self-mastery.

When you open to receive Spirit Guidance and allow the soul lesson to be realized, and follow that by actively practicing the insight in your waking world, when the next life test comes, your reward is to receive a beautiful crown chakra activation!

*"What is meant by a crown chakra activation?"* you ask. It is a widening of the aperture, a strengthening of the conduit, an expansion of the channel and a surge of Source power into your being—to give you more strength, energy and vigor, to give you greater depth and an ability to process and integrate information at a far greater volume.

You may find that the clarity of your thoughts is sharper, your intuition is greater and the guidance from your heart is more astute. The link between your body's intuition, your heart's guidance and your mind's acuity is strengthened greatly. Spirit Guidance is crystallized with the alignment of these aspects of your being.

This crown chakra activation is a Cosmic Upgrade!

So this is your reward for putting into action what you have learned from Spirit Guidance! Well done!

You are a fast learner and the mastery of lessons comes thick and fast now.

*Yes!*

**7 - 2**

# LIVE THE DREAM

D EAR ONE,

Currently there is a charge within—an active expansion of—your energy field. Your form is are surrounded by a spiraling golden translucent force field, in preparation for this chapter of your life, where you step into a role of great expansion.

In the light of imminent opportunity, doors are opening and there is a building sense of excitement mixed with the hope, like *"Heck, this is all going to work out!"*

And there is a reminder from Spirit here to envision how you would like it to unfold. In your meditations and prayers, entertain the reality of it working out *exactly* as it suits you—the more details the better. Write it all out if you need to, get very specific: dates, locations, numbers on the chart, distribution, people you want to meet etc. "Go for Gold" as Master Cannon would say. What does "Gold" look like in this next chapter of your life?

In the expansive, golden, translucent force field that you have successfully woven around your person from years of meditation—is pure, unbridled potential and creativity. It is almost as if it awaits your command…it is ready to be encoded with the vision of how you wish to manifest your existence. *This* is co-creation with Spirit. *This* is infusing creative potential with your intention that then shapes reality. And it is a marvel to watch it play out—conscious intention orchestrating reality in real time. *This* is directing the show of your life!

The important part of visualizing how you would like something to unfold—is to release any expectation or attachment to an outcome. If you remain rigid and locked on something happening a certain way, you will be disappointed. If you envisage and then *completely* release the vision and intention with no expectation—*total surrender*—you will be amazed and delighted and overjoyed as things miraculously fall into place the way you desired. *This* is Co-creation 101.

So while the information for new meetings are falling into place over the next couple of weeks, find a quiet space and take some time to write, draw, dream, and imagine the outcome you would like to create (in alignment with your highest good) and watch as magic happens…

The release and the surrender is the part where you let the Universe handle the details. You let the Universe form and actualize the experience from the place of pure potential—infused with conscious intention that has been released into the ethers… *this* is how Magic Happens. So this is a good practice for you! To claim your time to shine!!! Yeah, you—you have been laying the foundation bricks for a very long time! And you so deserve this!

So breathe that in! And let it be so! Any fears, doubts, concerns, or worries that it may all fall apart—acknowledge them and dismiss them because there is really no room for them in your field. Let us banish them together here and now—two powerful Sorcerers aligning with the same intention! Huzzah!

Yes…It is done. (With some zapping sound effects and a swirling vortex to add some bling!)

Rest easy. Sleep deep. Allow yourself to recharge for as much as you need to… because things are about to get busy. Don't stress about the past…it is time to restore and recoup and dream and recalibrate. Always when there is a lull in your energy it is time to regenerate and go within…

*Yes!*

# THE PROSPERITY OF DIVINE FLOW

EAR ONE,

*I am safe. I am loved. I am going with the flow…*

You can say this to yourself unto infinity throughout the day, as a mantra. At first it may be hollow words, but upon repeating them over and over to yourself you will find that you can infuse them with the emotional charge that creates them as real experience in your waking life. It is a practice!

You can literally *will* yourself to be in the divine flow. Just like meditation, harmonizing yourself into the current of the divine universe takes practice. First comes the will (which you have demonstrated), then comes the reoccurring intention and the practice…and then something goes *"click"*… and you start to notice little things. They creep into your experience and you find yourself delighted by magical, mysterious synchronicities in your waking world.

These moments of synchronicity present in your life when you least expect it and are like finding treasure. They are beyond comprehension because the magic and mystery of the universe puzzles the intellect and defies description. It is a whole-being knowingness rather than a conceptual understanding. And you know when you get a glimpse or a glimmer—at first the mind will doubt what it is seeing, because it is hardwired to the program and construct of your belief system.

It may be that you think of a person and they call you that instant. It may be that you have a dream and the memory of that dream returns and is triggered by something you see or smell or hear that day. It may be that you receive a symbolic vision and that vision is affirmed by finding that symbol in your waking life. It may be just inexplicable joy and gratitude. It may be the feeling of the presence of someone who has passed over. It may be a whisper in the wind. It may be the play of light in the water or through the leaves in the forest...Spirit is calling you. Spirit is guiding always. With the will and eyes to see, you can open up the aperture of your experience to feel the rush of LOVE that is available to you in all ways and always.

You will know when you are in harmony with the universe, because you will be in harmony with your spirit. Beyond the mind, beyond the body, beyond the emotions— is your radiant radical magnificent spirit...beckoning to guide you, beckoning to be synchronized with your whole being. My teacher calls this Harmonic Coherence.

It is a state of being where you are zinging. And it takes practice...

So be mindful that you don't beat yourself up for not getting it straight away. Have patience with yourself and the little child inside of you that wants to get it right and have it this instant because somewhere along the way it got hurt. This starts with the will and the intention, and this you have in plenty...

*Breathe.* Every time you do yoga, meditate, still your thoughts, take some time for self care, allow yourself to BE in nature—you consciously breathe and embody your spirit. You are practicing the art of being in harmony with all of creation. You affirm to the universe that this is your state of being and that you are ready to unlock the doors from within to receive the abundance and prosperity of the divine flow.

*Yes!*

# OLD WISE SOUL

D EAR ONE,

When life prompts you to say things like, "I feel like I am having a true awakening," these affirmative words generate a wave of power, a surge if you will, responding to your feedback.

This power surge is now being directed at you. You have created this. You have manifested this. You are the orchestrator of this wave. I truly hope you can recognize that. This is your doing and your creation. This is the universe responding to your willingness to open your mind and your having the courage to shine the light into the depths of your being.

So breathe deeply into this wave of power that is coming to you—you will feel it! It is the life force, it is affirmation, it is recognition and awareness. It is light, it is love. This infusion of energy is encoded with trillions of bytes of information that catalyze the "awakening" in your consciousness. It is an unfolding, a clearing, a revealing. It is the "aha" moment.

This is Recognition.

Before healing occurs, one must recognize the schisms, the discord, the fractures and fragments, the dissonance and the places of stagnation as patterns in their consciousness. Once the patterns of discord are recognized, we are able to direct conscious intention to transform these into patterns of harmony and resonance.

The beautiful thing about consciousness is its ability to shape-shift. It is malleable, acquiescent and able to change form. Consciousness has no limitations. It is not governed by space and time. Thus by envisioning and embodying the reverberation of balance, harmony, and equilibrium, our body will naturally fall into a state of alignment with the conscious intention to heal.

So first we have Recognition. Then we have Restoration, followed by Regeneration.

And now you are encouraged to access a piece of music, "Harmony of the Oms Sphères" by Patrick Bernhardt. Listen to this loudly or through head phones as often as you feel called, as it is literally assisting your consciousness to come into a state of harmonic resonance. In many ways, it filters out the energetic debris, vibrates it right out of your field...

This is preparation for opening the windows in your mind to bring in the light and the concept of fluidity. The fluid mind is free. The fluid mind is not rigid or locked in the regular parameters of the matrix. The fluid mind is adept at weaving the particles of consciousness to shape reality.

In this instance, the reality we are intending to create is one where you are vibrantly well. Where you are strong. Where you are fit, able and vital. Where the life force flows through with great gusto. Where, with your feet firmly planted on the ground and your mind open to the universal field, you walk with grace. You walk with ease. You walk with joy and laughter.

When you become conscious of the life force that animates your being, you are tuned into the power of the universe. You resonate with that power and you begin to flow with it, rather than create resistance. Life takes you on a course beyond your wildest dreams. Life takes you on a current of magnificent delight and extraordinary beauty.

Yes… Be awakened…. Be delighted…. Be joyful…. Be fulfilled…. Be saturated with the bliss of knowing that you are in harmony with all of creation. This is the ultimate human experience. The is the pinnacle of a life lived in gratitude and bliss. This is the holy Now….

You have it, my friend. You have this knowing inside of you. You have accessed the codes and activated your awareness to unearth the deepest aspects of your being with the conscious intention to heal, and it is unfolding before your eyes, through your body, a somatic and visceral response to this intention.

You now magnetize the people you need and the experiences to assist you ever onward, ever deeper—the orchestration of the light show that is your life, the random spontaneous particles of consciousness transforming your experience of reality to one of joy…

Joy is the reward for shining the light into the depths. Happiness is the reward for releasing old pain. Fulfillment is the reward for having the courage to examine the source wound. The multi-layered facets of the wound will reveal themselves in time. And you have set the wheels in motion by way of your willingness to receive. Your willingness to look. Your willingness to be open.

The domino effect is happening. The ball is moving. The die is cast. The cogs in the mechanism of the universal creation game are turning…

And where there is a spanner in the works, or a grinding in the gears, you will receive the awareness and the recognition to reveal it, to examine it, to feel what needs to be felt—and to let it go.

So you are off! And running! Or should I say gleefully dancing and skipping and waving a kite as you go. Your inner child gets it, completely gets it.

The one who chose all of this ahead of time gets it. Your spirit knew what it was signing up for: the parents, the lack of self-worth, the chink in the armor, the deep current of feeling misplaced, unworthy and unwanted…these feelings run so deep that they take you all the way into the Source of your heart.…

It is so magic and beautiful how your source wound generates the current that will lead you into the temple of your heart. Surrender to the current and there you will find yourself in all your glory…the I AM presence.

One with Creator. One with the Divine. One with Your Spirit. One with All. One.

One Love. One Source. One Consciousness.

Welcome home.

*Yes!*

# CONSCIOUS DEATH

D EAR ONE,

So beautiful is your state of mind, your ability to surrender, to mentally prepare yourself for what may or may not be…

I am so blown away by your ability to embrace the possibility of dying with such grace and grit, so much clarity and focus. You are a true champion, a light warrior and a hero in my eyes.

Not to say that there isn't a huge amount of emotion tied up in this possibility, but this is to acknowledge your state of grace, your level of mastery, and your incredible strength of spirit in the face of the ultimate challenge.

For all of us to be so lucky to have that courage and that sheer determination looking death in the face with such fearlessness and, dare I say it, charm.

Here is a poem I wrote many years ago…it feels pertinent to share it now:

> I saw death before it saw me,
> Caught it off its guard.
> Surprised it was that one so small —
> Defied its playing cards.
> "Shuffle them around again and
> don't stop 'til I'm through,
> of living this whole lifetime and
> THEN I'll deal with you."

So we stand with Death today. And we say, hang on a minute here, mate, this one is not done. They've got work to do—they're not ready to go and you need to take them off your list, for now. And then we ask for a sign from the universe that Death has heard this message. And we make an agreement here and now that you will be a great prize when that moment comes, because in truth, how many souls step through that door with full awareness, fully embracing the portal and the journey home? Not many. For the masses, they go blindly, fearful, fighting…but this one—when she is ready—will alight upon your step with full consciousness, full embodied wakefulness to dance across the threshold and this, my friend, is rarer than the rarest jewel. It is a gift to claim such a noble soul…when the timing is of her choosing.

So, dear Death, beloved cloak that forms the vessel to carry our spirits home, I beseech thee, make the moment of this one's own choosing. Let them define the magic that befits a King or Queen, a God or Goddess, a Master of the Great Mystery to take them home when they deem fit to call upon you.

That is my prayer for you today.…

And with the nod that I envision receiving by sheer will, the presence of Death steps back into the shadows…I hear the 'click' of a mechanism or latch that activates and allows a flood and an infusion of the life force. It is soft golden-white light flooding your being... pillows of pink fluffy clouds in a golden sunrise....

This is liberation from the paradigm of the ailing Mama and the maternal ancestors—freedom, strength, an eagle taking flight.

Restraining bolts have been taken off your spirit so that it can fly free—transform, transmute, shape shift, animagus, you are the Eagle. Strength, power, vision—this is your emblem. Watch for this in the coming days.

Be free, my love—the ultimate experience—spirit flies free while embodied in the flesh. This is Mastery!

Yes and with an accelerated processing beacon in your field—snap, kapow, whizz the information, codes and cellular memory of the matriarchy through in fast-forward motion as "Ave Maria," the song of forgiveness comes on. Please play it loudly and often over the next few days.

And upon looking up from the session I see the round setting sun peeking through two parallel clouds—God's Eye in the sky.

*Yes!*

# QUESTIONS FOR CLARITY AND FLOW

D EAR ONE,

The funk that you've experienced is universally felt right now. You are not alone—human beings are feeling the squeeze from all directions. We are in a pressure cooker of intensity and what has lain in the shadows for many eons is revealing itself for us to see...

And it is not comfortable because these feelings are murky and sometimes painful; but you, unlike most humans, are on the path of healing and on the path of recognizing all aspects of yourself no matter how weird, wild and wonderful...

In this way, you are so brave and so courageous because it is no easy thing to sit in the discomfort, to sit with the unease and the squirmy restless, shifting, wriggling and writhing feelings that present themselves. Most people numb out, self-medicate and do whatever they can to "not" feel the discomfort. Remember to keep breathing through the funk. Remember to allow the feelings to be there and to experience them. Emotions are like water—they travel in waves—so whatever you are feeling will pass. You can get swept up and tumbled and dumped by the wave, or you can let it roll right on past you, or you can dive under or up and over…or you can surf it!

How about riding the wave and using its momentum to carry you to the shore…the most exhilarating of these…

To do this, you need to be in sync with the wave. You need to know when to surrender to the current and when to give a push to be in the full power of its arc. There is a window of time that you are able to do this, or else you miss the wave and need to wait until the next one…

It is right timing. It is being tuned into the synchronicity of the universe and your existence in relationship to that synchronicity. Knowing when to push, when to surrender to the flow. This translates as when to talk versus when to listen, when to give and when to receive, when to be active and when to rest—all the while listening to the natural instinct of your body. Your body is a miraculous sensory instrument that knows how to ease into the sweeping momentum of the wave. When we tune in and listen to a body that is in alignment with our hearts and minds, it will guide us. It will give us signals and know when to give the push to catch the wave.

So all of these words and all of this information is coming through in an attempt to explain an experience that is available to you…one of being in harmony with the universe. One of being in surrender to something far greater than any of us.…

And we are funny creatures, because we get caught in whirlpools and eddies. In the mind-loops that go around and around, we are experts at beating ourselves up and chastising ourselves for how we are doing it wrong and what is not right or working.

Hold for a moment the thought that everything is exactly as it should be. Even in your funk. Even in the whirlpools and eddies, everything is unfolding and everything is so very appropriate…you are experiencing everything just as it should be. This thought brings you back into a place of acceptance and it allows you to be present once more with what is happening in a non-judgmental way. You are doing the best that you can. You are a human being having a human experience…

We are also in a time of filtering what serves you and what doesn't. Does your community serve you? Does the work situation serve you? Does your living situation serve you? Do your relationships serve you? What works and what creates an irritation? We are all being asked to look at the things in our lives that create abrasive energy in our field. We are filtering, sorting, shifting, refining and clearing out the stuff that has been creating drag, the stuff that has been bringing us down. The cosmic energy that we are receiving is helping us to ascend and evolve into a greater awareness of what it means to be alive. We are rising and the things that burden us and keep us bogged down have got to go!

So there is a feeling of letting go and sorting through the turbulent feelings to find our truth about any given situation.

Where does our passion lie? What do we really want? What is it we are here to do on planet Earth at this time? What gives us joy? What brings us fulfillment? All the while balancing the act of needing to pay bills and put food on the table?! Where is the happy medium?

In the wave! Riding the wave! So throughout this session, you may have felt wave upon wave rolling through your body, and it may indeed create the "flow" of emotions that want to roll on out of your body.

Where there was stagnation, there is now flow. Where there was a feeling of stuckness, there is forward momentum. This energy coming through to you may even take a few days to integrate, but it is carrying you forward in your life with a sense of acceptance and surrender...that you are exactly where you need to be and everything is exactly as it is meant to be. It takes the fight and struggle out of your field to feel this. It brings clarity to aspects of your life that were uncertain or confusing.

Where to flow next? How to flow and who to flow with? Who do you want to ride the wave with? Holding these questions in meditation will reveal many things. Your spirit will guide you.

These words of guidance come with a powerful spiral of energy into the back of your neck...a gentle but strong unwinding, a releasing of old mental constructs and habitual thought patterns that no longer serve you, a dissipation and dissolution of old ways of being in the world. It may feel uncertain at first as you test the waters and walk through the world without old familiar ways of thinking. We so often hang onto old ways of being because they are familiar and there is comfort in the familiarity, even though those ways of being are detrimental to our life force....

It takes courage to release the old paradigm. It takes courage to expand your awareness and step outside of the old costume—who you thought you were— when it no longer fits or serves you...

Spirit Guidance is giving you a pat on the back, my friend. An acknowledgement of commitment to your own transformation. This self-work goes largely unrecognized and unacknowledged because it is so very much about your unique and personal relationship to the divine. So here is your validation! Good job! Yay you!

Breathe that in, feel that wave, ride that wave and let it flowwwwwww....

*Yes!*

**7 · 7**

# TRUST IN YOUR AWAKENING AND BE FREE

D EAR ONE,

Let's acknowledge the delicate nature of what is in the spotlight here as you leap with trust in asking for help with matters that *appear* to be beyond your comprehension.

I want to place that trust on a beautiful soft velvet cushion and lay it on an altar of goodness—the highest good. You are asking the Divine for help, you are asking Creator, and that trust is a most exquisite and beautiful thing to behold. Strengthening the bond of relationship with God is an extremely private experience, and that is what is on offer here: the recognition of God within you, through you, *as* you...and an awareness that when you are aligned and in unison with ONE source consciousness, there is only the play and the orchestration of light and love and grace.

You have the power, the birthright, to claim your liberation and your freedom, and the only thing that can hold you back or box you in, is your beliefs.

A wise man once said to me, "The negative forces invade without invitation… but God respects free will and therefore awaits for a person to ask for help." And there is so much truth in that. If ever you find yourself stressing and fretting about a situation, call on the Higher Power to help you. Invite the presence of God into your house (your body, your mind, your spirit) and you will feel protected…you will feel the light and love that knows no bounds…

This Almighty Presence in your life is what is being cultivated now! Remember the nugget of goodness in amidst the intensity! You are cultivating a relationship…and Love reigns supreme. Love wins. Love heals all. God is love. Call Great Spirit into your heart and mind and you will begin to feel this as a palpable presence or guardianship in your life…

You have the power to do that, and ultimately it is up to you. We are all sovereign spirits, incarnate, experiencing life with access to the infinite power and glory of all of creation.

When the lights go on in inside your mind and you have an "aha" moment, this is when you will be free. This is when you will realize the soul lesson that has been fused to an experience. This is when you can have a breakthrough, break open the lock inside yourself and *know yourself as a divine being*. This is when you will **know** deep in your own bones that it is done. It is complete. And then you will not need any other outside perspective on the matter because it will be plain as day, as obvious as your own hand in front of your face.

This is the cosmic joke: you are looking outside of yourself to find answers but they are within you! It is your awakening, your blossoming and realizing and opening to the magnificent, glorious, powerful, and amazing being that you are! And in this awareness, you also realize that you are free. No other being can claim dominion over your soul. No other being can bind you, no matter the *ju ju* involved—this Earthly frip-frappery is small fry to the higher power.

It is experiencing yourself as a divine being—a spirit, incarnate—knowing you are one with all of creation—that you allow the love and grace and light to flood into your being to cast out all heaviness, all tangles thrown at us. With LOVE at your back shining the light on the path before you, there is also a deep, deep, deep sense of calm and peace that comes. You are free! There is transformation—in your cells, in your whole body, in your mind…

This is a transformation of the mind! So from now on, every time you find yourself stressing, fretting, worrying about something being done, call on the Higher Power of love and light to fill you, guide you. Breathe it in…until it is REAL and tangible, and it will grow and grow and grow with practice. Meditation is awesome, as is yoga, tai chi, etc.—any practice that has you be present and embodied.

You can't fake the realization and, with this spotlight on the relationship being cultivated, it is hard to doubt it. There will be signs, doors opening, synchronicities in your life that can leave you no doubt that this is the REAL deal. Glimmers at first—snippets and glimpses of total awe that come thicker and faster until they are the norm—because it is the all and everything that you are tapping into. And this is the great and bottomless well, the infinite source of protection, nourishment and healing.

It takes a brave soul to persist with firmness to ride it out, so pat yourself on the back for staying the course and trusting. There's that beautiful word again, TRUST.

Trust in the higher power, call on your angels. They are ready and here to assist you and guide you and protect you. It only takes you asking and they are with you.

And as for destiny? It is what it is and so it is appropriate. Everything is appropriate! All life experience is valid! Could it have been done differently? Maybe in a parallel universe it played out in a different way, but in this one—here and now—this is what is happening. So it is real. There are jewels to be found in amidst the hardship and soul lessons to be learned in the experience of intensity. You chose to master those lessons in the Game of Life at the Great Mystery School, and you are right on track!

When an unsettling experience arises, consider that perhaps your soul would not evolve without this experience.

You continue to find your way on the path of your destiny and everything is exactly as it should be!

Call in the grace of The Beloved, awaken to your remarkable spirit, and be free!

*Yes!*

# AFTERWORD

D EAR ONE,

You are waking up. You are coming out of the darkness and into the light. You are remembering Who You Are as Divine Being—beyond all of the judgment, the self-loathing, the shame and the despair. You are waking up from the nightmare that is your current reality and remembering that you have the power to create your life in alignment with your heart's desire, your heart's calling. You are waking up to the possibility that you are worthy of a life that is beautiful. You are remembering that your inherent nature is joy, wonder and delight and you are reclaiming that.

You are reclaiming your true power as a sovereign being. You are reconnecting to your Self and you are being guided by that light, that connection, that Source. You are remembering yourself as one with God/Goddess/Creator/Beloved/Great Spirit/Allah/ Jehovah, the Supreme Being—whatever your name for the Higher Power.

This great reclamation starts with your intention: *the will*, your focus and your ability to direct your thoughts and consciousness to align it with the affirmative. This is a life affirmation. You are affirming life! You are choosing life! Sometimes events appear to trigger you, and then you forget this and become bogged down in the mire of misery and self doubt and angst and despair; but there is always the light—the dancing, sparkling, flickering light that catches your attention and reminds you that there is always a way.

"Where there is a will, there is a way."

These times of great change—these times where the unified field is apparently dominated by fear—is an opportunity for the strengthening of your will. You are flexing the muscles of your willpower to consciously drag yourself out of the mire in your own life and shine like a beacon, as living example of *Love*.

*Love* is the answer. *Love heals all*. When the mind, the body, the spirit are in alignment, you are able to receive this Spirit Guidance. Your spirit is always guiding you on the path to live a life of triumph and victory where *Love* is the guiding force. *Love reigns supreme* in harmony with your Divine Nature and in harmony with Nature, Mother Earth. This is synchronicity. This is equanimity, homeostasis and equilibrium.

We are *Love*.

We are One with the Source of all Creation, one Consciousness, one Reality.

Before colonization, First Nations lived in harmony with Mother Earth for thousands of years in reverence, respect and gratitude for the bounty that allowed them to live life. We must learn from them how to be an Earth Steward, how to pray to the ancestors, how to give and receive food and water without tipping the balance. Every single indigenous culture has its rituals, ceremonies, rites of passage, stories, dances, songs and language that weaves an intricate web of knowing one's place. In modern civilization, we have become lost—we have lost those traditions that support and guide us. Yet as we awaken, we are remembering our place in the grand cosmic scheme of things, we are remembering ourselves and our part in the great web of life. As we reconnect to Great Spirit and the Dreamtime—and remember that we are spirits incarnate—our own Spirit Guidance will show us how to live and BE the bridge between Heaven and Earth, how to walk in balance, how to remember who we are, as Spiritual Warriors, standing strong in our truth, with free will, mastering the self and surrendering to the Higher Power.

We are learning how to *Love* ourselves. We are helping each other. We are all equal. No one is above or below another. Some are just further along the river. We are all equal before God.

As we remember, as we awaken. We magnetize others who are in alignment, whose vibration matches ours. Friends will come and go as those that no longer resonate will vibrate out of our field. Let those that no longer match your vibration go.

So my prayer for you, dear One, is to have courage—courage to align your will and your conscious intention so that you can find your way home to yourself. This—for you to remember that you are one with all of creation and deserving of *Love*, and that you are *Love* and that you are *Loving* in all ways and always. My prayer is that you know that you are worthy of a life that is rich and fulfilling. And that through it, you find joy delight, contentment, synchronicity, magic and wonder.

This book has been about Remembering: remembering yourself as a spirit, remembering your part in the divine order of things, remembering your will and your place, in alignment with your true nature—that is, *Love*.

And with that comes more confidence than you can ever dream possible.

"As within, so without."

"As above, so below."

Fill the cup to overflowing so that everyone you see, meet, or otherwise encounter is saturated and enchanted with this pure bliss nectar of *Love*...

# ACKNOWLEDGMENTS

MANY SOULS DESERVE MY devotion and respect for their guidance and teachings in reaching this place of peace in myself. I would like to introduce them to you in the order of our soul meetings.

My parents, Dr.'s Maggie and Bill McLeod, are worth a book in their own right for the way they have taught me to see and feel and experience life with both scientific curiosity and a deeply inquiring mind. Their life's work is the about the Art of Transformation and their passion has always been about where science and mysticism meet. It was recently in my own healing journey that I realized I continue to carry the torch forward and brandish the flame of their life's work in my own way. With this recognition, I felt an incredible force of power at my back, like an invisible hand of support behind me.

My sisters and brother, Liz, Fi and Andy, are all rock stars in their own ways, doing amazing things with their lives. Liz is a paediatric surgeon saving the lives of children on a daily basis. Fiona is a high-profile barrister. Andy is an architect who designs and creates sustainable, energy-efficient buildings of exquisite beauty that connect people to nature and one another. It is with great pride that I speak about them to others and call them my kith and kin.

The next stands out as my "go to" when the lessons of life are all consuming, Master Charles Cannon, an ordained monk of the Vedic Order of Sannyasins, the oldest existing monastic order in the world today. His teachings and guidance have been instrumental in my journey of self-discovery and ultimately the liberation of my radiant self. He is quoted throughout this body of work, his voice and his guidance coming through in the sessions and bringing with it the wisdom from the lineage of that orthodox, Vedic Tantric tradition. I consider myself lucky and blessed to call him my friend, my teacher and guide. Since the inception of this book, he has left this Earthly plane. Before he died, he gave me his blessings for this book. I can't help but feel that his Spirit is flowing through me as I continue the work.

And there is my beloved Branden, who has devoted his life in service to our family and to healing the planet and an environmentalist, advocate and activist. His love and affection has allowed me to dive deeply into my own healing journey with no boundaries. His dedication and commitment to all that he holds dear is a remarkable testimony to what an amazing human being he is and I am deeply honored to share my life with him. It is his love and devotion that has allowed me to be all that I am.

Our children, Ruby and Xander, whom I love with all my heart, have been my greatest teachers and inspiration. It is an honor to walk with them in this life and I am so proud of who they are! Their presence in my life, completes me and gives me purpose, like nothing else on this Earth.

And I'd like to make special mention of my dear friends, Celia Costarella, who is my rock and "other mother" to my kids and has been by my side through so many deep waves of healing; Mary Morris, who has been there with me for many years, encouraging me and believing in me; Nicki Tostevin, who has assisted me to bring my vision to life; Amy Galland, whose kind wisdom and council have always been so welcomed; my mother in-law, Dorothea Adamson, who always believed in me; and Laura Paradis, for holding space for my family.

I would also love to acknowledge Mary Barber and Sara Whiteford, two soul sisters and such dear friends. One of their greatest gifts to me was to spread word of my work, enabling it to flourish and bloom. There's also the mother/daughter team of Linda Klein and Lillon Anderson for holding loving space for me to grow and evolve this work to be where it is at!

I thank my dearest friends Pete and Rue for your part in my family's lives. Mary Frank for your wise council. The Ortiz family for your loving and kind support through an international move. Patrick Harestad for our shared time in sacred space. Una Viggiani for your biz savvy and ability to hold space for me to pull it all together. Wyliam Holder for your infinite kindness and care.

And of course, Penelope Love, poet, author and weaver of magic with the written word. It is incredibly hard to describe in words, what I see. And she has taken this stream of consciousness and put it in a readable form! And I would like to acknowledge my beloved Patreon supporters (not mentioned above and at time of print): Paula Redman, Ashton Whittington., Rohini Moradi, Domonique Echeverria, Betsy Streeter, Jo Gumbley, Vineeta Jane, Heidi Calderon, Kimberly Ardwell, Mindi Smith, Maheen Adamson, Steve Greening, Wyliam Holder, Connie Holt, Tina Davidson, Jonathan Frieman, and Domonique Echeverria.

There are many healers who have assisted me to find wholeness. Those who wish to remain anonymous, you know who you are. There is also Alberto Martinez and all of his ancestors, who guided me through the darkest night of the soul, to whom I am grateful for the restoration of my life force and the liberation of my spirit, assisting me to be here, in service to others. There is Anthea Amore, for her love and generosity when my body was so broken; Kerry Brown and Kris Franken, for being my Aussie Soul sistas; Sandra England, for her wisdom and council over the years; and Peace Mother Geeta Sacred Song, the Mayan Shaman who shared her wisdom with me.

Finally I would like to acknowledge the First Nations of South America, North America and Australia, as well as my ancestors in the United Kingdom. Much of my healing has been born from indigenous teachings, and I am forever humbled by the wisdom keepers and elders who hold the knowledge of our divine nature and remember the ways of living in harmony with Mother Earth.

Lastly I give thanks to all of the elders, healers, mystics, and visionaries that have paved the way and planted the seeds before us.

In love and gratitude, that I may be the conduit, in service, to the awakening of another soul…

# ABOUT THE AUTHOR

**Sarah McLeod** is an artist, activist, director and healer. She is the founder of Vision Weaving: The Art of Transformation, and her passion is the evolution of consciousness. She weaves healing through ritual, art, theatre, film and private sessions and is devoted to assisting people in spiritual awakening. She has an international clientele and her healing work and artistry through music is streamed and distributed to a worldwide audience. The energy transmission embedded in her unique brand of lightwork began to form with the guidance of her teacher and the lineage of the Vedic Tantric tradition. It was then fashioned and birthed after many sacred ceremonies with indigenous elders and enables a profound reconnection to source. For more information, visit www.VisionWeaving.com.

# Publisher's Note

Thank you for reading *Spirit Guidance*. Please pass the torch of connection by helping other readers find this book. Here are suggestions for your consideration:

- Write an online customer review wherever books are sold.

- Gift this book to friends, family, and colleagues.

- Share a photo of yourself with the book on social media and tag #sarahmcleod and #spiritguidancebook.

- Bring in Sarah McLeod as a speaker for your business, club or organization.

- Suggest *Spirit Guidance* to your local book club.

- Recommend *Spirit Guidance* to the manager of your local independent book store.

- For bulk orders, contact the publisher at +1-828-585-7030 or email Orders@CitrinePublishing.com.

- Connect with Sarah McLeod at www.visionweaving.com.

Your book reviews, social media shares and emails are received with heartfelt gratitude.

Made in the USA
Las Vegas, NV
27 November 2020

11573221R00143